Spell-a-Day™

Spell-a-Day™

Lead a Charmed Life All Year Long

BARNES
&NOBLE
B O O K S
NEW YORK

This material originally appeared in
Llewellyn's 2001 Spell-a-Day Calendar.

Copyright © 2000 Llewellyn Publications

This edition published by Barnes & Noble, Inc., by
arrangement with Llewellyn Publications.

All rights reserved. No part of this book may be used
or reproduced in any manner whatsoever without
the written consent of the Publisher.

2000 Barnes & Noble Books

ISBN 0-7607-2330-3

Text design by Lundquist Design, New York

Printed and bound in the United States

    01 02 03 04 M 9 8 7 6 5 4 3 2

BVG

Contents

Key to Signs and Symbols

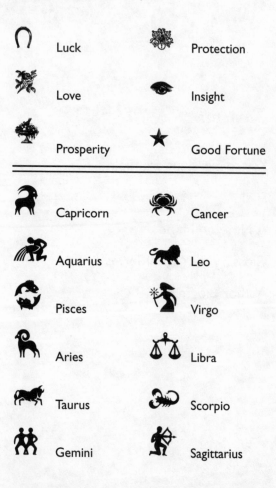

	Luck		Protection
	Love		Insight
	Prosperity		Good Fortune

	Capricorn		Cancer
	Aquarius		Leo
	Pisces		Virgo
	Aries		Libra
	Taurus		Scorpio
	Gemini		Sagittarius

January 1

New Year's Spell

To ensure that your life is blessed with good luck through the next twelve months, perform this simple spell at midnight on New Year's Eve. First, open every door and window of your house to allow the spirit of the old year to depart. Go outside and light a green candle that has been anointed with a few drops of cinnamon, cypress, or lotus oil, and, without uttering a single word, reenter your house through the backdoor. Walk through every room with the candle in your hand, go back outside through the front door and then in again by the back. Additionally, you may place a silver coin, a piece of coal, and a piece of bread on a windowsill or porch at midnight on New Year's Eve, and then bring them into the house after you rise from bed on New Year's morning.

Gerina Dunwich

2 January

Stone Power Spell

To create a spell of power using stones, during the Full Moon place one adventurine, one carnelian, and one smoky quartz in a bowl of spring water and set outside so that the Moon is reflected in the water. Say these words: "Here on the day of Mars, in the hour of the Sun, I call down the Moon to charge and energize these stones!" With your wand in hand and arms upraised, dance around the bowl chanting repeatedly: "Power of Luna, Power of Sol, Power of Aries, Power I call!" When the energy level is highest, grasp the wand in both hands and point the wand at the bowl: "Empowered Be!" Drain the water into a jar and store for use as a power elixir. Remove the stones, wrap each in black cloth, and put away until you need an extra power kick in spells and charms.

Ann Moura

Smell-the-Flowers Spell

Have you ever driven a long way and arrived only to realize that you were traveling on autopilot and missed the trip? If so, try this spell during your next journey. As you climb into your car, say aloud: "As I travel, Mercury, let me be here, let me see, mind awake and eyes alert, tales to tell, so mote it be!" Now pretend that you are going to report on this trip later. Look for items worth telling about—a giant cottonwood, for instance, its age, its history, its size and beauty; or a dilapidated old house, and the shrubbery that covers it and makes it seem spooky. Keep discovering new items until you have collected nine, then rehearse them in your mind. If you forget any, make sure to find something to replace it.

Amber K

4 January

Prosperity Ribbons

To promote prosperity, gather three feet of emerald green, royal blue, and metallic gold ribbon. Tie the three ribbons together at one end with three knots, then start braiding the three ribbons. With each turn, see yourself prospering and then becoming generous with your new wealth. When you are finished with the braiding of the three ribbons, tie three knots at the end. If you can get a gold or silver band, slide it onto your newly braided cord of ribbons. Finally, take the two knotted ends and tie them together with three more knots, thus forming a circle, containing a total of nine knots. Keep this ribbon circle in your bedroom, as it also can foster love.

Lori Bruno

Cajun Love Spell

Try this Cajun Love Spell only if you really want to steam up your love life. Women: Use a white linen handkerchief with lace trim or embroidery. Men: Use a plain, white cotton handkerchief. To begin, wash the handkerchief in sea-salted water. Rinse thoroughly, and iron with starch while it is still slightly damp. The handkerchief should be fairly stiff. Next, jog in place to work up a good sweat, then fold the handkerchief diagonally (point to point) one time. Fold the triangle in three, and pull back the points to fashion a flower, or fleur-de-lis. Take the flower-handkerchief and gently swab the sweat from your body, especially under your arms, where pheromones are most strong. Lightly spray the handkerchief with sandalwood perfume. When you next see your lover, use it to wipe his or her brow. Bury the handkerchief in the Earth during the next Full Moon.

Marguerite Elsbeth

6 January

A New Year's Wish

At the beginning of the New Year or just after Yule, gather together a garland and some small candles. Using the garland, create a spiral on the floor and surround it with the candles. If this is included in a group ritual, create a grouping of three spirals like those found at Newgrange in Ireland. Walk the spiral as you would a labyrinth. Pause at the entrance to visualize what you wish for the New Year. Begin your walk at a pace that feels right, repeating the incantation: "With each step I take, with each breath I create, let my spirit awake for this wish I make." Once you reach the center, step over the innermost boundary of the spiral and verbalize your wish. Retrace your steps out of the spiral, repeating the incantation again.

Sedwin

Anticold Spell

My grandmother used this recipe as a spell to get rid of colds.

Chicken Soup
- 1 whole chicken (about 3–4 pounds)
- 2 onions
- 3 carrots
- 4 stalks of celery
- 5 cloves of garlic
- 6 pints water
- 2 teaspoons salt (or more to taste)
- 1 teaspoon fresh or ½ teaspoon dried parsley
- 2 teaspoons sage
- 1¼ teaspoons rosemary
- 1 teaspoon thyme

Cut the onions into eight pieces, and the carrots and celery into four pieces. Put everything in a four-quart pot, boil and simmer one hour. Drink a cup of broth hourly. Eat the solids when you feel like it.

Magenta Griffith

8 January

Call-Me Spell

If you are waiting for someone desirable to call you, try this spell. First, sit with a picture of the person or visualize the person clearly in your mind. Sing to yourself: "Call me. Don't be afraid. You can call me. Call me and I'll be around." After a few minutes, release the energy into the universe and go about your business. Don't wait by the phone because the "I'm not being called" energy will interfere with your psychic call for a call.

Therese Francis

Family Spell for the New Year

To tap into family energy, take a red and a green candle and write down the things you are thankful for and that you intend to accomplish through this New Year. As you burn the candles, meditate on your resources, your family, and support network. How do they help you accomplish your goals, and how do you help others in accomplishing theirs? Burn the paper while releasing any leftover holiday blues and then cook something fun for yourself. Look around your home—perhaps there are little things you can do to make it more cozy and comfortable. Clean up any leftover holiday clutter.

Estelle Daniels

10 January

A Spell to Improve Communications

Often, relationship problems are caused by a lack of communication. In order to fight this, light two white votive candles while thinking of your estranged friend or family member. Imagine the person surrounded by a flame of protective light. See yourself surrounded by another flame of protective light. Then see the two flames move toward each other and become one flame with both of you inside of it. Be still for several minutes. Do not attempt to talk to the other person, but listen carefully to see if the other person says anything. Blow out the candles. Know that you will be able to talk to each other about your relationship soon.

Therese Francis

A Spell for Releasing Outcomes

Sometimes we are so worried about the outcome of an event that we tense up and close our minds to success. We sabotage the very result we seek. Try this spell for letting go of expectations. First, gather some rocks to hold in each hand—either two large stones or two handfuls of gravel. Then, chant to yourself:

> Blessed be the powers above.
> Let me know your trust and love.
> I know what will be, will be,
> And I trust you'll take care of me.

As you speak, clench your fists around the rocks, then open your hands. Imagine letting go of your needs and fears as the stones drop. Wash your hands in running water, and say the rhyme once more.

Amber K

12 January

Love Powder

To make a potent love powder, place some plain talc in a small bowl and leave in the moonlight before a Full Moon. The next night, add seven drops of geranium oil, seven of ylang ylang oil, and three of patchouli oil. Again, leave in the moonlight. On the third night add one more drop of each essence, concentrating on the enchanting and transformative power of the Moon-drenched powder. Visualize it glowing with the power to bewitch any who come into contact with it. Place the powder in tinfoil to keep it fresh, and wear or scatter a little whenever you desire to attract love.

Kala Trobe

Capricorn Energy Spell

For a spell to tap into the Capricornian urge to build, you will need an 8½ x 11-inch piece of graph paper and a pencil or pen. Write down as specifically as you can what it is that you wish to build. Include also the boundaries that must be set, and the foundation that you need to create. Draw the symbols of Saturn (♄) and Capricorn (♑) on the paper, then write a list of your ancestors on the back of the paper. Each day, fill in one line of boxes by coloring them in with colored pencils as you burn your favorite incense. Repeat your intentions mentally or aloud as you work on the paper. After you complete each line, fold the paper into a square and place under a bowl that contains salt and dirt. When your desire manifests, bury the paper, the salt, and the dirt in your backyard.

Silver RavenWolf

14 January

Delilah's Delight Hair Spell

Each night, as you brush your hair, focus on brushing out tension and brushing in radiance. The first few moments should be to relax and massage your scalp, and to detangle your hair. Visualize loosening the tension from the day as you do this and sliding it out of your body. Then, as you become more relaxed, see every stroke of the brush imparting a crackle, a radiance to your hair, making it shine and so making you shine. As you brush, softly repeat: "Hair that gleams in gentle streams, make of me a glowing dream. Hair that falls when sirens call, let my inner beauty beam."

Yasmine Galenorn

Moon Garden

To create a Moon garden in even the smallest apartment, create a special area with pots on a terrace or window ledge. (You can also do this in your garden, if you have one.) In the center of this area place white stones or crystals to form a circle. Surround the circle with plants that have silvery leaves or white flowers such as lamb's ears, dusty miller, and cyclamen. Plant mugwort in each of the cardinal directions. Use your Moon garden for Full Moon rituals and meditation. Place an offering of different sacred objects in the center of the circle during Full Moons, saying: "Dear Sister Moon, shine on me with peace and power. So mote it be."

Sedwin

16 January

Barrier Removal Spell

For this spell, play strongly rhythmic music as you build a wall around yourself out of children's blocks, boxes, or whatever is handy. Think of this wall as a boundary that exists in your mind and restricts you from feeling free. Turn slowly within your wall and contemplate this boundary. Ask yourself if this boundary is not just a product of your own fear of change. Feel the fear build within you, and, when you are ready, firmly and decisively break down the wall. Dance freely and wildly outside and around your broken wall, as you resolve to accept new freedom in your life. When your energy peaks, ground some of it by kneeling to touch the ground and giving thanks for your power to change. Conclude by saying, "With harm to none, so mote it be!"

Maria Kay Simms

Seeing Gremlins

When you are in an airplane flying on a moonlit night and you are in a window seat, fix your gaze out on the wing, and look for slightly brighter spots of moonlight glistening off the metal. These are likely air elementals, a subspecies of the "gremlin," who have come along for the ride. Forgetting Hollywood's ridiculous film portrayals, you should know these creatures are usually well-intentioned, if occasionally a little mischievous. If you have some second sight, it is likely that you will be able to see them walking across the wing, or sitting on the leading edge with their little feet dangling in the wind, enjoying the ride. Send them blessings and good wishes in your mind—they can be enjoyable company and useful friends later!

Ed Fitch

18 January

Spell for Success at School

In order to promote good performance on a test or other school project, after you have finished all your studying put your notes under your pillow, and put the textbook or books under the head of your bed. This will not substitute for studying, but it will help you to understand the subject even more than otherwise. You may dream of the material. That's okay. It is possible to gain some useful insights through your dreams.

Magenta Griffith

January 19

Recycling for a Vision of Love

The drippings from the candles you use in your spells and rituals can help divine who your future love might be. Save them and when ready melt the bits of wax in a pot until the mass is liquefied. Pour a good amount of the melted wax into a bowl of cold water. As the wax cools in the water, it will take on a unique shape. Let your mind go free as you look at the hardened wax figure, much as you would while watching clouds on a lazy summer day. The wax will form a shape that will reveal something about your future love. A sailor may be represented by an anchor, a fisherman by a fish, or a banker by a money sack. While this rite may not bring your future love to your doorstep, it may help you to look in all the right places for your heart's fulfillment.

Gwydion O'Hara

20 January

Three Goddesses Spell

In a north German tradition, the Sun, Moon, and Earth were revered as three sisters called Borbet, Ambet, and Wilbet, or "the Three Eternal Ones." These sisters were granted powers over the human mind, soul, and body. To invoke the blessings of these three goddesses, go out into your garden and tie gold, silver, and green ribbons around the branch of a tree near your door while chanting:

> Three sisters fine, three sisters fair,
> Accept my love and hear my prayer.
> Bless one and all who pass by here.

Janina Renée

January 21

Getting Rid of a Cold Spell

Sometimes, no matter what we do, we can't avoid the worst of winter's viruses. To help get rid of a cold, start by bringing some water to a boil. Add fenugreek seeds to the water while chanting: "Seeds of fortune, seeds of change, restore my body." Continue to boil the water and seeds for five minutes, then remove from heat. Strain the water and sip the tea. You should not add sugar or honey to the tea, but lemon is fine.

Therese Francis

22 January

An Olive Oil Blessing For New Appliances

Olive oil has long been associated with the ancient Greek goddess Athena and with magical blessings. Use this charm to consecrate new appliances around the home. Place a drop of olive oil on your finger, then trace a personal holy symbol—perhaps a cross or pentagram—on a hidden part of the appliance while chanting: "I bless you with this sacred oil to help me with my endless toil. Make use of powers of earth, fire, water, and air to serve me well. Blessed be!" You may bless any appliance in this manner—microwaves, toasters, and the rest.

Jim Weaver

January 23

Being-in-the-Now Fashion Ritual

You've gained weight and have three sizes of clothes in your closet. While comfortable with yourself, the sight of these smaller versions of you makes you queasy. What to do? Try making a cleansing ritual out of it. First, try on all of your clothes and divide them into three piles: those that don't fit, those that fit but that you don't like, and those that fit and you like. When your closet is empty, smudge the space with jasmine incense. Visualize lovely, well-fitting clothes hanging there, then hang up those clothes that fit. Of those that fit but you don't like, decide what you must keep due to budget. The rest, along with the clothes that don't fit, you will bundle off to the nearest thrift shop. Now, your closet is ready, clean, and waiting for you to fill it with new clothes.

Yasmine Galenorn

24 January

Dragon Spell

To dispel all negative vibrations and bad luck, place a small jade dragon upon your altar and anoint it with a few drops of cypress or lotus oil. Light some dragon's blood incense and place it in a fireproof burner to the right of the dragon. To the left of the dragon, light a new black candle that has also been anointed. Take the dragon in your hands and, as you concentrate upon your intent, pass it clockwise through the smoke of the incense nine times. Nine is a magical number that symbolizes completeness and the highest attainment of achievements on both a mental and spiritual level. After you have done this, return the dragon to the altar and recite the following incantation: "Let this dragon spell be made this hour to keep me safe from harm. Negative vibrations fade by power of the dragon's charm. So mote it be!"

Gerina Dunwich

January 25

Five Pennies Spell

Your front door functions as an ideal place for inviting energies of prosperity into your home. To do this, place five shiny pennies beneath your porch. This will encourage both money and love to enter your household. A bit of food under the porch will ensure that you will never know hunger, too.

Scott Cunningham

26 January

"Too Sexy" Oil

Going out on a Saturday night? Use these oils to bring out your sexy side. For women: 2 drops patchouli oil and 3–5 drops lotus oil, or 1–2 drops patchouli oil, 2 drops sandalwood oil, and 3–5 drops lavender oil. For men: 2 drops patchouli oil, 5 drops orris oil, and 2–4 drops sandalwood oil. For both men and women: 2 drops patchouli oil, 3–4 drops sandalwood oil, and 1–2 drops musk oil. To wear these oils, mix with a few drops of neutral carrier oil (such as almond or jojoba). It's best to mix up a fresh batch each time. For extra *oomph,* mix or apply oil during the hour of Venus or mix on Friday. Charge the oil by passing it through the smoke of patchouli, cinnamon, sandalwood, or rose incense. Wear with black clothing and silver jewelry. Smashing!

Denise Dumars

Sacred Space Spell

To create a sacred space, take paper and pen, a white candle and lighter, a metal bowl, and a mirror, and sit down in a place of your choosing. Light the candle, place it in front of the mirror, and gaze into its flame. Gradually visualize your own image behind the flame. Imagine it aging, and recognize this image as your elder self, your high self. Ask this wiser being a question about a problem that has been bothering you, and listen carefully for a quiet voice of conscience to speak to you. Receive words of wisdom about the spiritual solution for your problem, and write your promise to take this advice. Catch the edge of the paper in the flame, offering your pledge to the spirit. Drop the flaming paper into the bowl, and offer the ashes to the south wind.

Maria Kay Simms

28 January

Spell for Depression

Depression distorts a person's outlook on life, but the following spell can help you see things differently. To begin, as the Sun rises hold a golden ring up to the dawn-glow. (Or, if you have a view of a low horizon, where you can look directly at the Sun for the first few seconds without hurting your eyes, you can hold the ring up to the Sun disk.) Looking through the ring, visualize a stream of golden rays flowing in through your eyes, suffusing every cell in your brain and every atom of your being, as you say, "I am filled with golden radiance!" Rise on nine mornings and watch the Sun come up nine times. Overcast days do not count, but get up anyway, to salute the eastern quarter. Note: This spell should be combined with proper medical treatment if needed.

Janina Renée

Spell for Ending Nightmares

At the end of the day as your child is getting ready for bed, you can help create a psychically safe space for her to keep nightmares out. To start, have the child stand next to her bed. Rub your own hands together briskly until they tingle, and starting at the top of the child's head, move your hands down the outside of the child's body about three inches from the surface. Imagine a blue shell enclosing your child in safety as you do so, and have your child imagine the blue shell, too. Then have the child make a blue shell for you.

Therese Francis

30 January

Garlic Protection Spell

For a good dose of protection, get a whole bulb of garlic. Cast a circle if you wish. Hold the bulb of garlic in your hands and say: "As this garlic is whole, and yet made up of many parts, let my house, made of many parts, be whole." Divide the bulb into cloves, and put one over each door and window of your house. No evil will pass the garlic to enter your house.

Magenta Griffith

Protect a Vehicle

To protect yourself when using a vehicle to travel from place to place, every time you get into a car, bus, train, or airplane, imagine that the vehicle is surrounded by a bubble of blue protective light.

Therese Francis

1 February

Prosperity Spell for Children

To bless a child with long life, good health, happiness, and prosperity, when a child loses its first teeth place them in a small clear gold-tinted bottle. Along with the tiny teeth, place in the bottle a few rose petals, some angelica and orris root, several cloves and a cinnamon stick, some rue and vervain, and a piece of gold and a piece of silver. The gold and silver need not be fancy—even a small earring will do. Put each of the child's first teeth in the bottle until you have collected them all. Then, blow some of your breath into the bottle, and say: "Long life, good health, happiness, prosperity, and love." Seal the bottle with red wax.

Lori Bruno

February 2

Earth Mother Candle Ritual

Imbolc is a time of year when many people celebrate change and growth, and bid farewell to things no longer needed. For this spell, sweep a circle with a broom to symbolically remove the old to make room for the new. It is also a tradition to burn candles on this night as an offering to the Earth Mother so that her divine power of fertility may soon awaken from its winter slumber and bring forth springtime. Light a green candle and recite thrice the following incantation: "Mother Earth, awaken from your silent winter rest. Let the springtime goddess of green magic manifest. Mother Earth, awaken now and hold us to your breast. We honor thee with love, for we are truly by thee blessed."

Gerina Dunwich

3 February

Conversing with the Spirits

If you wish to revisit a passed-on loved one, this is a rite that may open the doorway between the realms. On the anniversary of the departed one's death, go off alone and light three purple candles and one black cat candle figure. Arrange them on a table with a mirror and turn out the lights. As you sit before the mirror and candlelight, call out the departed one's name over and over as if chanting a sacred mantra. After a time, you will see the spectre of the departed one behind you as you gaze into the mirror. Continue chanting, and you will hear the spectre's voice as if it were your own thoughts. When the spirit has said all that he or she wishes, the spectre will disappear. Afterwards, extinguish the candles and thank the spirit aloud for heeding your call. Take flowers to the resting place of the departed as a gesture of gratitude.

Gwydion O'Hara

February 4

Circle Amulet Spell

The circle symbolizes both the Sun and the arche-type of the self. These are astrologically appro-priate, for Sun signs represent self-expression. Carl Jung thought it was important for people to meditate on symbols of the self, but in modern life many of us lose our ability to do so. Therefore, an important addition to anyone's collection of mag-ical jewelry is a circular broach or pendant. If you have such an article, charge it with the following spell to recall you to your self. First, hold the item to the light of the noon Sun as you recite: "In this round, myself am found; whole unto myself, at one with the circle of power and creation." Then, wear this amulet when feeling tired or ill, to invoke the restoration that comes through reconnection with the deep self.

Janina Renée

5 February

An Olive Oil Blessing for the Home

You may blend olive oil and water in this spell to make a perfect ritual for cleansing and blessing your home. To begin, during the waxing cycle of the Moon combine a teaspoon of olive oil and one quarter cup of water in a small bowl. Stir in a clockwise direction with your finger. Starting at an east-facing door or window if possible and moving about your home in a clockwise direction, begin sprinkling the mixture with your fingers as you say: "I bless this house, this space, every hearth, window, and door; protection surrounds this place, now and forever more." When finished, respectfully discard the remaining mixture by pouring it down a drain or sprinkling in your garden. Repeat this blessing ritual whenever you feel it is needed.

Jim Weaver

February 6

ABC Protection Amulet

To make a protection amulet, during the third or tenth hours after sunrise, or the first or eighth hours after sunset, sew a small pouch from black cloth and red thread. Place three herbs in a cauldron, and speak after each: "Agrimony to return negative energies to the sender. Blackthorn to deflect negative energies away from me. Clove to exorcise harmful energies from my presence." Stir with the tip of the ritual knife, and recite: "Three herbs I call to work for me, harnessing negative energy. Take and bind and send away harmful forces in my way." Put the herbs in the pouch, sew it up, and set it on a pentacle. Wave your wand and touch it to the pouch. "Earth and Air, Fire and Water! Emanations of the Lady and the Lord! I call upon thy grace and love to seal protection in this ward!" Carry it in your pocket or purse.

Ann Moura

7 February

Aquarius Energy Spell

To promote freedom, you may turn to Aquarian energy. To start, gather thirteen ribbons of any color, a bag of buttons, and needle and thread. On a Wednesday, sew as many buttons as possible on each piece of ribbon, saving about two inches at the top. When you have finished, tie or sew the ribbons together at the top, and hold your hands over your work as you state your intentions. Make the sign of Uranus (♅) and Aquarius (♒) in the air over the project, then take the ribbons outside and hang them from a tree, porch railing, or other spot, as you say: "From heaven to Earth, from Earth to heaven, the winds circle about my desire, carrying my thoughts to the gods of the universe and returning with the gift of positive abundance. So mote it be." Allow the project to hang outside until your wish has been granted.

Silver RavenWolf

Spell for Fun and Surprises

For a spell of fun and surprises, treat yourself to an outing with a young person, and go to the movies, have lunch, and hang around the mall. Be flexible in case of the unexpected. Burn a yellow or golden candle and meditate on children and how they are important to society. Send love and peaceful energy to the children of your neighborhood and those who care for them. Have fun while it lasts, and don't harbor regrets.

Estelle Daniels

9 February

To Ease an Unrequited Love

When the torment of a love unaccepted and un-returned weighs heavy upon the heart and soul, you may choose to purge it with fire. To start, kneel before a blazing fire with a handful of dried vervain leaves. Toss the entire handful into the blaze at once along with the words: "Creature of fire, flames that roar. Purge me of pain, let it torment no more. Consume the hurt, that my soul is set free. As I will, so mote it be!" As the fragrance of the herb penetrates the air, breathe it in deeply, and visualize your entire being filling with peace and calm.

Gwydion O'Hara

If Wishes Were Fishes

To help realize a wish, visualize yourself doing something you've always wanted to do. Then, light a small candle and chant: "I wish a thing, a thing to be. I wish a thing, a thing for me." While holding the candle, chant this verse nine times. Keep your visualization as vivid, active, and detailed as you can. Blow out the candle. Watch as your psychic energy goes out into the universe to make your wish happen.

Janina Renée

11 February

Spell for Fertility Within a Relationship

To promote spiritual, mental, or physical fertility within a relationship, during a waxing Moon work with your partner to anoint three red and two green candles with rose oil, rubbing from center to tip and center to base. Know that when they are lit, the candles will signal the beginning of the abundance of your mutual choosing. Talk positively as you work, and take turns lighting the candles while laughing. Then, each person should hold a pomegranate for a moment, and imbue it with your aspirations. Pour some pink champagne into a copper vessel, split the pomegranate, and drop the pips into the vessel. Say: "May each seed take root and flourish as we desire." Using your fingers, take turns placing seeds in one another's mouths until all are gone. Finally, drink the champagne and end the spell with frolicsome activities of your choice.

Kala Trobe

February 12

The Home Treasure Book Spell

For finding a new home, or for redecorating an old one, it can be beneficial to keep a three-ring binder and divide it into sections, one for each room of the house you'd like to have, one for the house itself, and one for the land surrounding the house. Use a paper punch to punch holes in paper to insert into the binder. Each time you find a picture of a house you like, a piece of furniture you like, or something that evokes the mood you would like to have in your home, cut it out and paste it into the proper section. This gives you a focus, raises your energy, and helps you define what it is you are looking for in a home.

Yasmine Galenorn

13 February

A Lemon Cleansing

To cleanse a place of any ill-intention or negative energy, use two fresh lemons. Cut the lemons in half, and anoint the skin with cleansing oil. Place one lemon half in each corner of the room to be cleansed. If the need is great, the lemons will turn black within a day or two. When they do, toss them out knowing that the ill will is vanishing with them. In extreme cases, the lemons may turn black within a matter of a couple of hours. If this is the case, it may be wise to repeat the rite a second time to collect any remaining negativity.

Gwydion O'Hara

February 14

Valentine's Day

A Valentine's Day Love Spell

Valentine's Day is the ideal time of the year for women and men to perform love magic. To attract a new lover into your life, draw a bath during any of the Venus hours of this day (7:00 am, 2:00 pm, or 9:00 pm). To the bathwater add a handful of rose petals and six drops of music oil. (Six is a magical number ruled by Venus.) To enhance the spell, burn love-attracting incense such as African violet, cherry, cinnamon, gardenia, ginger, hibiscus, jasmine, lavender, lotus, rose, strawberry, or vanilla. Surround the tub with the flickering flames of pink candles and then fill your mind with romantic thoughts as you bathe and whisper the following rhyme: "Lover hear me call to thee. Let these words enchant and draw. Lover find your way to me. Love is the magic, love is the law. As it is willed, so mote it be."

Gerina Dunwich

15 February

Binding Spell for Lovers (A Spell for Lupercalia)

The roots for Valentine's Day are in an ancient Roman holiday named for wolves. Wolves mate for life, and the Romans believed that Lupercalia, February 15, is the day they chose to select their partners. To strengthen the ties that bind you to your life's partner, anoint each other's body during a waxing Moon with a potion consisting of any of the following: hair from a dog to connect with the wolf's energy, damiana to enhance sexual stamina, rosemary or mullien to promote lasting love, vanilla or apple blossom to create romance, willow for binding, and yerba maté for friendship. As you anoint various points on your lover's body, renew the vows you've made to each other according to your shared vision for your life together. There are as many ways to love as there are lovers.

Edain McCoy

February 16

Come Hither Spell

Do you wish your lover would come closer? This spell may help. To start, on a Friday night just before a Full Moon place your favorite rose-quartz crystal in a clear glass filled with purified water, and put it outside under the moonlight for several hours. Pour half the water into a small, white bowl, and leave the other half in the glass. Set a pale blue candle in the bowl, and light it. Place photographs of you and your lover in front of the bowl, and write your names, enclosed by a heart, on a piece of white paper. Drip the Moon water onto the images and names, with the intent that your lover will come to you. Drink the Moon water in the glass, and let the candle burn until the water extinguishes the flame.

Marguerite Elsbeth

17 February

Four Elements Spell

The four elements play an important role in magic and spirituality. You can increase your success in both by studying the powers of fire, water, air, and earth. Take a few moments to center yourself, then act out each of the four elements in turn. Use whatever sounds, gestures, and motions that make you think of that element. Don't worry about how you look or sound; think instead about how you feel. Sense the currents of energy flowing through you and feel how each element has its own unique signature. As you move, chant this verse: "Like a fire, leap and burn; like a river, whirl and turn; like a breeze, blow strong and sure; like a mountain, long endure." End by thanking the elements for their help. This spell has no specific time requirements but it does work better outside. It adapts well to group use as well.

Elizabeth Barrette

A Healing Puppet

For a healing spell, construct a puppet stuffed with chamomile flowers and vervain to represent the ailing person. Draw a black circle on the puppet where the ailment is concentrated. Consecrate the puppet, and place it on your altar, visualizing the individual in vibrant health. Then, put the puppet away. At the Full Moon, consecrate a straight pin and fill it with healing energies. Taking the puppet in your left hand, and the pin in your right, pierce the black circle with the pin. Concentrate all your willpower on healing the ailing individual, saying: "In the name of the God (or Goddess) I hold dear, I pierce this disease with the spear of healing. As the Full Moon wanes, so shall this ailment fall to nothing. So mote it be!" Leave the pin in the puppet and store it until the night of the New Moon, or until the person is restored. Then remove the pin and disassemble the puppet.

Gwydion O'Hara

19 February

Find a New Home Spell

To find a new home, gather everyone who will live in the new home for this ritual. First, light a blue candle and calm everyone. Then chant "We now live in the perfect home in the perfect neighborhood." If any doubts or thoughts come up, say the word, "thought." Imagine the thought going into the flame and burning up. The released energy will help you continue your chant. After several minutes, speak the chant louder. Imagine the energy becoming a tornado moving upward into the universe to find the perfect home for you. Release the energy into the universe, knowing that you will be guided to the perfect home.

Therese Francis

Will Spell

To strengthen your will, stand at the bottom of a steep hill. Call upon the energy of the Earth, reaching deep into her center and feeling her energy flowing up through your feet and throughout your body. Take three deep breaths, and begin to climb. When you arrive at the top of the hill, turn slowly clockwise three times and look at the view, as you offer thanks to the Mother, to the universe, and to the power within yourself for your discipline and will in reaching the top. Breathe deeply, reflecting on what you have accomplished and what you will now be able to accomplish. Feel the energy of Earth beneath you, close your eyes, turn slowly clockwise three times, and look down at the ground. Find a small token from the Mother to take with you as a reminder of what you have learned about yourself.

Maria Kay Simms

21 February

Spell for During Mercury Retrograde

Every day that Mercury is retrograde, light a teal or silver-colored candle and meditate on how you want your life to be and what you want to do over the next three weeks or so. Wait until Mercury goes direct to actually start any of these new projects.

Therese Francis

February 22

The Merchant's Spell for Selling Things

Before you sell merchandise, you must give things away freely. That is, give to people three things: a clean and cheerful shop, plenty of sunlight, and a song. If people still don't buy as quickly as you wish, then cleanse yourself physically, emotionally, and spiritually, and wear turquoise and carnelian clothing. For still better sales, give three more gifts: a smile, a warm handclasp, and a spoken wish for a wonderful day. To increase sales further, say this rhyme to yourself:

> Bargain for both, when you tarry awhile,
> Fair trade, square trade, handshake, smile.

If you wish to sell still more, give away more: Sympathy for troubles, good will, and a story of hope. If you are still not selling, give up on the chocolate-dipped pickles and try opening a pizza place.

Amber K

23 February

Myrtle Crown Spell

Venus, the Roman Aphrodite, has as her symbol the evergreen myrtle. If thoughts of love are distressing you, make a simple crown of myrtle to make romance more possible in your life. To begin, take a piece of bendable wire and gently shape it around your forehead. Connect the ends at the back. Then bind strands of myrtle around the wire. If fresh myrtle is not available, use silk myrtle available from craft shops. Speak these words when you place the crown on your head: "Venus, goddess of love, as I wind this sacred fillet I wind away fear. I bind love to me. Venus venerandum, she who must be revered, may I make no sin against the laws of love, and may I be loved in return." Wear the fillet when you feel that love has got the best of you, or when your relationships are not working well.

deTraci Regula

February 24

Potpourri Spell

Make a potpourri of fresh pine needles, cedar chips, juniper berries, and other evergreens. Be sure to thank the spirit of any plant from whom you gather. Add whole cloves, cinnamon sticks, whole allspice, a sprinkle of gold glitter, and a few drops of the oil of one of the ingredients for extra scent. Meditate as you work on positive steps you can take in your world to increase your prosperity. Call on the spirit and feel it flow through your hands to charge the mixture. Put a bowl of this potpourri in your home and carry a small amount folded in a bit of cloth in your wallet. When the potpourri is no longer fresh, bury it in Mother Earth, giving thanks for the abundance she has given you.

Maria Kay Simms

25 February

Morning Aura Wake Up

On a dreary, sleepy morning on which you feel you'll never get started, rub your hands together until they tingle. Then, starting at your head, imagine rainbow-colored energy coming out of your hands and flowing over your body. Move your hands over the front of your body from your head to your toes. Starting again at your head, pull the energy down your back to the back of your feet. Again, starting at your head, pull the energy over your right side, then over your left side. See yourself enclosed in the rainbow-colored egg of healthy energy.

Therese Francis

February 26

Moon Brew

Set a silver container filled with water out on the night of the Full Moon just as it rises. Allow the water to soak up lunar rays all night, then just before dawn, rise and retrieve the water. Place the water in an earthen jug and cork tightly. Use this brew to anoint money to increase wealth. Touch it to your brow to promote psychic awareness. Or place it in the bath prior to lunar rituals to become attuned with the spiritual planes.

Scott Cunningham

27 February

Initiative Spell

Today, focus on taking the initiative and asserting yourself in all and any matters. Play recorded music with a strong drumming rhythm. Carve a red candle with appropriate symbols of your goal, such as Mars, Aries, fire, and the runes Ken and Tir. When you are finished carving, call to your favorite warrior goddess or god within, light the candle, place it in the center of the room, turn up your drumming music, and dance around the fire. Feel the beat throughout your body, and as you do, meditate on your intent and see yourself achieving it! When your energy peaks, throw your hands high into the air and shout: "Success! Success! Success!"

Maria Kay Simms

On the Road Jinxing Spell

A common form of "self-jinxing" occurs when you make an error and become so rattled by it that you make even more mistakes as a result. This is particularly unnerving when you do something improper in traffic such as accidentally running a stop sign or making a questionable turn in front of a police officer. To break such a spell, it's a good idea to find a convenient place to pull off the road and find something to divert your mind for a least ten minutes. If there are gift shops near by, consider stopping to buy a yellow candle in honor of Mercury, god of travel. Take it home to burn as a spell for clear thinking on the road. If you wish, inscribe it with the "R" rune Rad.

Janina Renée

29 February

Cardinal Flower Love Charm

The Roman goddess Cardea reigned over all things that opened and all things that shut, including hearts. The root of this plant serves as an irresistible force to unlock the mysteries of romance. It loves older ladies, and that works especially well for them. Simply gather the root at dawn, naked, standing on the left foot, and touch the root to all parts of the body. Chant as you do this: "May my love's heart open wide, and let my love dwell inside."

Verna Gates

Money Custard

Rich, delicious foods like this custard are ideal for a ritual money-making diet. Try this recipe especially.

Custard

    2 eggs
    1 egg yolk
    1¾ cups light cream
    ¾ cup granulated sugar

Beat eggs and yolk, and cook in a saucepan with cream and sugar, stirring until custard coats the spoon. Remove from heat, and place pan in a bowl of ice water. Stir occasionally as the custard cools. Eat small amounts as you visualize your coming wealth.

Scott Cunningham

2 March

Love Mist Spell

To create an elixir of love mist, fill a spray bottle with water and gather Venus oils—such as rose, geranium, cherry, ylang ylang, or vanilla. Draw a pentagram on the ground or floor to work within, and place drops of oils into the water until you are pleased with the scent. Ideally, work outdoors beneath Venus, the first bright evening star. If this is not possible, visualize a dark sky and focus on the brightest star. Raise your hands toward the light of that star and feel the flow of the goddess of love. Bring down her power and let it flow from your hands into the scented water. Put on the spray cap, and spray straight up into the air letting the lovely scented mist drift down on you. Spray mist as desired to charge areas and yourself.

Maria Kay Simms

Persephone Returns

One of the most well-known maiden goddess stories is of Demeter and her daughter Persephone. Persephone felt that it was her calling to go to the underworld to comfort and guide the spirits of the dead to their rest. Even though Demeter knew her daughter would return, she put her life on hold and waited. Because of Demeter's inactivity, the weather was cold, and grains and plants did not grow in the fields. When Persephone returned, bringing warmth and love for her mother, the Earth came alive again. At this time of year, the Earth is renewing herself. Signs of reawakening are everywhere. Honor the goddess by baking bread or by leaving an offering of grain in your favorite outdoor place. Take time to reflect on your winter journey. Plan your path into summer with fresh challenges to help you grow. This season of planting is also for spiritual seeds.

Sedwin

4 March

Diffuse Sorrow Spell

To help diffuse personal sorrow and transform it into useful energy to enliven your environment, mix your favorite incense with the yellow petals of St. John's Wort (or with the powdered contents of a St. John's Wort capsule) in a small bag or pouch of lightweight cloth. Wear this close to your body, envisioning depression and sadness as a blue mist being drawn from your body and into the pouch. Once a day, burn the contents in a brazier as you chant: "Sorrow flows out and away, dispersed in ether, transformed in flame. Blended with incense, may it bring pleasure." If you wish, carry the incense burner outdoors to let the smoke be further dispersed by the winds. Continue this spell for as long as you deem necessary.

Janina Renée

March 5

Pisces Energy Spell

Passionate Pisces helps us to step out of the daily humdrum. To tap into this energy, place a dry sponge in a bowl. Mix some patchouli oil and water in a resealable container, then write one statement on a piece of paper that announces the way you wish to use the Pisces energy. Place the paper under the bowl, slowly pour the patchouli water over the sponge, and say: "Like this sponge, I will soak up (your intention)." Place a white rose on top of the sponge. Hold your hands over the rose, breathing deeply, and mentally touching the unconditional love of the universe. When you are finished, with your hand draw the sigils of Neptune (Ψ) and Pisces (♓) over the flower and bowl. After one week, wring out the sponge and offer the rose to free-flowing water. Repeat this spell once a week until you have reached your desire.

Silver RavenWolf

6 March

Safe Dreaming Spell

Sometimes when we wander in our dreams, we have nightmares or find ourselves facing daunting energies on the astral plane. We can alleviate some of these encounters by warding our bedrooms thoroughly and by keeping charms with us when we sleep. In this spell, stuff into a 5 x 7-inch pillowcase two parts mugwort, two parts hops, one part lavender, one part chamomile, one part rosemary, and one-half part frankincense. Then, add three small polished moonstones and a piece of aventurine to the mix. Sew or tie the pillowcase tightly so the herbs don't spill out at night. This should promote restful sleep and ward against nightmares.

Yasmine Galenorn

Safe Flight Spell

The night before leaving on an airplane, take a ring, watch, or other piece of jewelry that you will be wearing on the flight. Hold it in your hand, and imagine the plane surrounded by blue protective light that starts at the nose of the plane and moves to the tail. Imagine the light extending off each wing and keeping the entire airplane working perfectly. Then, imagine the light helping the pilots focus on the flight and keeping everyone inside the plane safe and calm during the flight. Put on your seatbelt when you get into your seat on the plane. Again imagine the blue protective light around the plane. Then sit back and enjoy your flight.

Therese Francis

Lightning Spell

When a thunderstorm is raging, fix your mind on what you truly and sincerely wish for and watch the lightning each time it flares. Concentrate more and more intensely—with a chant if you can—then just as a particularly brilliant or close lightning bolt splits the sky, send your wish forth!

Ed Fitch

March 9

Purim

Spell for Your Body

For a spell for your body, burn a green or white candle while meditating on your health, and how you can improve your wellness. You may think about steps as simple as taking a multivitamin every day to starting a whole body workout plan with a diet change or anything in between. If you take care of yourself, life will feel better. Identify stress makers in your life and make a plan to cope with them better. Just identifying stress and telling yourself you can cope and deal with it is half the battle. Release any built-up stress as the candle burns. Reward yourself with a bubble bath, massage, or makeover, and feel how good your body can be when you take care of yourself.

Estelle Daniels

10 March

Decision Spell

When you're having trouble deciding among alternatives, place one chair for each choice within your ritual area, and label each chair with one of the choices. Now center yourself and create sacred space around you and your chairs. Call on Mercury and the goddess Minerva to aid you in making your choice. Sit in a chair, and explain to the other chairs why the chair you're sitting on is the best choice. Be assertive, defend your position, and give every reason you can think of for this particular choice. Switch chairs and repeat for each one. At some point in the debate, one "chair" will make the most sense! That's it! Your magic has worked! Thank the deities and carry out the winning alternative knowing you've made the right choice.

Maria Kay Simms

March 11

Athlete's Foot Relief Spell

To cast a spell for athlete's foot relief, add twenty drops of rosemary essential oil or one quart of rosemary tea to hot water in a dishpan. Light a red candle, and soak your feet in the hot rosemary water for ten minutes while imaging that, as the candle burns down, the fungus on your feet is going away. When finished, dry your feet. Pour the water down the drain. Then blow out the candle. Repeat twice a day for five days.

Therese Francis

12 March

Flood Protection Spell

To protect your home from flooding, sprinkle salt or salt water in every room of your house, repeating this incantation: "Water of river, water of sea. Brigid, Holle, Astarte, keep harm from me." Visualize white light moving clockwise around the outside of your house (or neighborhood), enveloping it with protective energy.

Sedwin

Increasing Physical Endurance and Focus Spell

The night before doing anything that requires a lot of physical endurance, such as running a marathon, light a white candle and a red candle. Focus on the flame from the red candle. Feel the heat from the flame flow into your body, providing you strength and endurance. Then focus on the white candle flame. Feel the power of the flame flow into your mind, providing you with calm focus. During your athletic event, remember the feeling of the flames within you, providing you focus and strength. Caution: Spells augment, but do not replace, training. Only use this spell if you are adequately trained for your athletic event.

Therese Francis

14 March

A Spell for Communicating True Love

If you want to let someone know you love them, first meditate deeply on your feelings and discover whether your love is pure. True love exists when you love someone just as they are, and ask nothing in return. If you want them to change to suit your needs, then your love is not pure. But if your love is true, cast a circle and write words akin to these on a parchment scented with rose or pine: "Please know that I love you just as you are, and I ask nothing in return. Should you ever need a friend, I am here for you. I say this once, and not again unless you wish me to. I love you." Sign in blue (the color of honor), and send it. Give thanks for the opportunity to love, and expect nothing more.

Amber K

March 15

Business Loan Spell

If you are hoping to facilitate the process of getting a new business loan, you may want to try this spell during the waxing phase of the Moon. Using a pencil, inscribe a bayberry candle with the amount of cash you need to borrow. Then light the candle and chant something like: "Candle light and fire, bring me my desire. Bring me everything I need by wing and foot with lightning speed." Allow the candle to burn down completely.

Dorothy Morrison

16 March

Aradia Love Spell

You can bring your lover to you by asking the Italian Fairy Queen, Diana, to call upon her daughter, Aradia, for aid. Choose the first Thursday following a New Moon and plan to stay awake all night to think only of your lover. At dawn, call your beloved to you when the Moon is still visible and the Sun is just rising, saying: "Good and beautiful Diana, I have faithfully worshiped you; now help me! Call your daughter Aradia, and send her to fetch my love to me. Fill our souls with the joy of lovemaking. Thank you, great Fairy Queen and fair Aradia." Dogs are sacred to Diana, so if the tryst must be kept secret, your lover may come disguised as a dog, shape-shifting into human form only when you are alone.

Marguerite Elsbeth

March 17

St. Patrick's Day

Weather Lore

According to the ancient beliefs, the turn of the Moon brings a change in the weather. This means right after the New and Full Moons are the most likely time for the weather to change. Furthermore, if the Moon is bright orange when it rises, the weather will be warmer the next day. And a ring around the Moon means snow is on the way.

Magenta Griffith

18 March

Antibody Bath

Run down? Try this spell. First, wrap a few tea-spoons each of dried or fresh bay leaves, rose-mary, and thyme in a square of material such as cheesecloth and tie to the hot tap on your bath-tub. Run a bath through it, strip, add some salt and visualize the water glowing white, the steam cleansing your aura. Now add several drops of rosemary oil, picturing it in green and red fortify-ing your aura against interloping bacteria. Finally, add the ginseng, saying: "I am wholly fortified against all ill." Imagine an outwardly permeable bubble of protection surrounding you, your anti-bodies, like watchmen, alert to any impostors. Treat yourself to a cup of cocoa or milk in bed, and have an early night.

Kala Trobe

Rain Song

This is a traditional rain song often sung as a table blessing. If you don't know the tune, you can chant the words. Hold up a glass of water or apple juice as you chant to give the spell extra power. The more people who sing this, the stronger the magic.

> The Lord is good to me,
> And so I thank the Lord,
> For giving me
> The things I need
> The sun, the rain, and the apple seed.
> The Lord is good to me.

Therese Francis

20 March

Seed Blessing Ritual for the Spring Equinox

The Spring Equinox is a traditional time for many Witches to perform blessings over the seeds which they gathered in the fall of the previous year, though store-bought packets of seeds may be blessed as well. Perform the blessing at sunset in the center of a clockwise-cast circle. Place the seeds to be blessed in a basket or cauldron. If the seeds are contained within a packet, place the entire packet of seeds in the basket or cauldron. Using an athame or wand, thrice draw a pentagram in the air over the seeds, and say: "As winter's reign comes to an end and spring brings warmth and light, the spirit of these seeds I do call forth on Ostara's sacred night. From your rest awaken now with birth! You shall, in time, grow green and strong in the soil of Mother Earth. So mote it be!"

Gerina Dunwich

Computer Printer Spell

If you rely on your computer, you want to make sure it keeps running smoothly. This blessing bestows some magical protection on your precious equipment. For this you need two things: a computer-shaped puppet (you can buy plush computer toys in many stores, or make your own) and a clear plastic container large enough to hold the puppet. Name the puppet after your computer and touch it to each part of your system, then charge it by saying: "Clear screen and true colors, trouble-free memory and data, chips and disks, fleet-running programs and applications, knife-sharp printer and clean paper—all the system now secure!" Place the puppet in the container, and seal and store the container near your computer. Repeat periodically to keep sufficient energy in the protective field.

Elizabeth Barrette

22 March

Eat to Succeed

Adding to your prosperity can be as simple as whipping up a cup of coffee. The following food items can help increase your prosperity. Coffee: Mars loves it, and will help you fight boardroom battles; add cinnamon and nutmeg to enlist Jupiter's help as well. Gingerbread: Spice it with clove, nutmeg, cinnamon, mace, black pepper, and allspice. Indian Chai tea: contains the same spices and is a good substitute for coffee, both magically and in the culinary sense. Basil, galangal, and coriander: These spices are often used together in Thai food and have very exotic yet Jovian properties. Sage: Added to Thanksgiving stuffing, it's a digestive aid as well as a prosperity herb; add a pinch to blackberry tea or cobbler. Mint: There are many types of mint, and all are magical; buy a blend such as Moroccan mint tea to drink at work and serve to customers.

Denise Dumars

March 23

Choosing Between Two Lovers

If you are fortunate enough to have to choose between two lovers, during a Full Moon hold a lump of variegated quartz crystal while contemplating your dilemma. Consider the qualities of each party in turn and gaze into the crystal. Then lift the quartz skyward and say: "Isis bless me with accurate intuition." Put the crystal in a black pouch and add several cardamom pods, saying: "Anubis guide me through the labyrinth of my subconscious." Finally add a small white feather, first dedicating it: "Maat of balanced judgment, help me choose what is of most benefit to all." Place the pouch under your pillow. You will dream the solution.

Kala Trobe

24 March

A Dung Ball Spell

The Egyptians used scarabs in many ways—as amulets, decorations, and seals. Khepera was the beetle-formed god of the Sun, who rolled his eggs in a ball of dung. Most of us feel we have enough dung in our lives already. To help cope with this detritus, take a small lump of air-drying clay or potting soil and form it into a ball. Think about all of the "dung" that surrounds you, and press these thoughts into the ball. Let this dung ball dry, and when it is ready, think again on the dung that you put into it while you were forming it. Take the ball with you to a place away from your home and hurl it against a wall, fence, or cliff side. As the fragments scatter, know that the dung will no longer clutter up your life.

deTraci Regula

March 25

Sun Power Spell

To take advantage of the power of the Sun, go outdoors and greet the sunrise by stretching tall and wide. Take three deep breaths, inhaling the light and power of the Sun and exhaling them back out into the world. Realize that as the Sun is the center of our solar system and all of the planets reflect its light, so are you the center of your world, and all others around you will respond to your light. Resolve to shine brightly on this day, as you say: "Hail! I greet thee, radiant Sun; pour forth thy light on me. I will shine with peace and love toward everyone I see!" (If this day is cloudy, you can always visualize the Sun, knowing that the light is within!)

Maria Kay Simms

26 March

Clear Thinking Soup

For a soup that promotes clear thinking, gather the following ingredients:

Soup

    3 medium onions, chopped
    2 heads of garlic, chopped (about ¼ cup)
    2 tablespoons olive oil
    2 cups water
    1 carrot, chopped
    1 celery stick
    Chopped thyme, basil, parsley, dill, bay leaf

Cook onions and garlic in olive oil on medium heat until tender. Inhale the fumes, feeling them opening your mind to new ideas. Bring water to slow boil. Add cooked onions, garlic, carrot, and celery. Cover and simmer for 20 minutes. Add the herbs to taste and simmer covered for another ten minutes. Remove from heat and eat.

Therese Francis

Purification Spell for Fire

From inspiration to passion, fire energy can certainly excite your magical work. After lighting any candle, needfire, balefire, bonfire, or hearth, you might try this easy incantation: "Fire makes the magic go. Inner peace begins to flow. Rise, O flame and purify; enchant this place, ground to sky." For added strength draw the sigils for Leo, Sagittarius, and Aries on a pot, cauldron, or candle, or in the dirt at the south quarter of your circle. If you choose to boil a liquid in the pot, add the symbol for Scorpio. If you are really in an artsy mood, draw a salamander along with your other chosen sigils. Herbs and incenses placed on the prepared fire will add a puff of scent when lit, or you can wait and throw your herbal mixture into the fire at the peak of your spell or ritual.

Silver RavenWolf

28 March

Shield Spell to Protect an Important Letter

When a letter absolutely has to get there safely, you may use this shield spell. To start, take a leaf from a rowan tree, or a needle from a pine, and if possible enclose it in the letter. If you cannot reasonably do this, rub the leaf or needle on the address. On the upper right-hand corner of the front of the envelope, where the stamp will go, draw a small shield with a bar sinister (a bar going from lower left to upper right of the shield). Cover it with a large, brightly colored stamp (if you have a choice). In a strong voice, say to the letter:

> By Mercury, Hermes, and Thoth, I charge
>   thee:
> Horse and hattock, plane and truck:
> Go, and go, and go,
> Nor stop till thou have reached the hand I
>   intend.
> So mote it be!

Mail the letter and relax.

Amber K

Crystal Spell

To bring about something you truly desire, in the evening lay a crystal on some black cloth as you meditate on the powers of the ancient gods. Settle down in the near-darkness and fix your gaze on the crystal, willing power into it. Take your time, and eventually it will begin to glow, perhaps dimly or more brightly, with a white, green, or gray mist about it. Then pick up the crystal and rub it between your hands, drawing its power into your body. Then put down the crystal (your hands are likely to be glowing by now), wait thirteen breaths as you build the power even more and shape it to your desire, then throw the power forth with your hands. Afterward, light a candle or turn on the lights, and wash both your hands and the crystal in cold water to remove any residual glow.

Ed Fitch

30 March

Attracting Love Spell

To attract love you need one pink candle, one teaspoon of ground almonds (for happiness), and one teaspoon of rose water (to represent love). On a night leading up to the Full Moon, light the candle and relax. Sprinkle the almonds and rose water around the base of the candle and say the following: "Candle pink, warm with fire, bring to me the love I desire; with these almonds around the flame, Cupid's arrow will take aim. With this scent of fragrant rose, I bring this love spell to a close." Gaze into the flame for a moment. You may see an image of your new love. Let the candle burn out. Wait at least one lunar month before repeating.

Jim Weaver

March 31

Fairy Charm

Fairies are little nature spirits, found in many different forms around the world. They can be helpful or mischievous, depending on their type and how you treat them. This charm attracts friendly fairies to the area; they may bless your house, help your plants grow, or otherwise add a little sparkle to your life. You will need a crystal prism (of quartz or leaded glass) and some glitter. First wash the prism in plain water and chant this verse over it: "Fairies from afar, come to where the rainbows are; spread your blessings all around. Be safe and warm and welcome here, every season, every year. May our love and magic abound!" Now hang the prism in a window where sunlight can reach it. Go around your house and yard, sprinkling a pinch of glitter wherever you want to attract fairies. They will soon arrive.

Elizabeth Barrette

1 April

Trickster Spell

Nearly every pantheon has a Trickster figure; most cultures also have an "upside-down day," when people play pranks and make fun of normal life. In America, April 1 (or April Fools' Day) offers an opportunity to honor the Trickster figure. For this morning spell, do everything backwards. If you usually wear a robe, wear street clothes or go nude instead. Cast your circle in a direction opposite to the normal one. Put your candles in upside down, unlit. The invocation is backwards too; read it in a funny voice: "Tricksters of the world, begone! Today is a day of serious work, so stay far from all that I do, and teach me nothing of your ways. Depart now, amidst a hail of curses!" As you go through the day, wear one article of clothing backwards or inside-out in honor of the Trickster, and remain open to whatever lessons come.

Elizabeth Barrette

Bay Laurel Wreath for Abundance in the Home

To create abundance in the home, make a wreath of bay laurel. To start, bend eighteen inches of copper wire into a circle and tie the ends together. Attach strands of bay laurel—which can be bought from a florist shop—to the wire, and tie whole cinnamon sticks, small bags of cloves and mustard seeds, and ribbons of royal blue, emerald green, bright red, and metallic silver and gold to the wreath. If you wish, you may incorporate the images of the God and Goddess in this wreath. When your wreath is completed, say: "Wreath of abundance, with blessings from the gods, bring to this home health, wealth, prosperity, and love."

Lori Bruno

3 April

Lemon Cleansing Ritual

Now and then we all make the decision to eat better, start exercising, and get more sleep. It helps if we perform a ritual to jump-start our resolve. On the night before you begin your new regime, bring sixteen ounces of pure bottled water to just below boiling in a pan. Add two tablespoons of honey and dissolve it completely, then remove the water from the heat and add the juice of two lemons and one mint teabag. Cool the brew, remove the teabag, and pour everything into a glass jar into which you have placed a thoroughly scrubbed clear quartz crystal. Set in the sunlight for two hours to absorb the healing rays of the light, then remove the crystal and drink while focusing on strengthening your willpower and your desire to change and better yourself. Know that you truly love yourself in order to make this effort.

Yasmine Galenorn

April 4

Spell to Appease Family and In-laws

In a perfect world, we all would get along with our family and in-laws, but of course things don't always work out that way. To appease troublesome family members, anoint a small black candle with cypress, eucalyptus, or rosemary oil, and say: "Clarity, cut through the fog of hate." Imagine the candle as representative of your troubles. Know that as you watch, negative emotions will diminish. During a free hour each day light the candle, chanting: "Suspicion dwindle like this candle, meanness vanquished. Trouble calmed and spite appeased; you and I are at ease." Imagine the hostility melting, and light taking its place. Repeat at the same time every day until the candle is used up. Bury any fragments that remain far from your home. You may need to be persistent with this spell; family prejudice can be obdurate. Repeat as necessary.

Kala Trobe

5 April

Full Moon Chalice Spell

Two nights before the Full Moon, fill a chalice with clear spring water and place a solid silver coin at the bottom of the chalice. Carry the chalice outside and let it stand with the coin and water in it, and let the light of the goddess Diana, the Full Moon, shine on the cup. Meditate upon the abundance coming into the chalice, and feel the energy as you hold the chalice in your hands. Then, drink the water and feel the abundance and prosperity enter you as you say: "Goddess of the Full Moon, I ask you to grant me wealth and prosperity, that I may live in comfort, and return these gifts to humanity." After the ritual, keep your coin in a silver lamé pouch.

Lori Bruno

April 6

The Right Love Spell

Are you uncertain about your present relationship? Do you want to know if your lover is Mr. or Ms. Right? If you are up to learning the truth about your lover, try this love spell. Take two silver coins, and throw them up into the air, saying: "If this love is right, make it stay so; if this love is wrong, let my love go." Watch the coins carefully; should the coins fall close together, or if both coins land heads up, the love is true. Should the coins land far apart or tails up, you may separate in time. One head and one tail indicates a rocky road with much separation and reuniting along the way. If the coins land on top of one another, you will be married before the year's end.

Marguerite Elsbeth

7 April

Spell for Relationships

To bring magic to your loved ones, you should consider relationships not just with your spouse or partner, but with your doctor, lawyer, accountant—anyone you have a one-on-one relationship with. To begin, burn a gray candle and think how your relationships with people affect your life. Release any negative feelings and maybe determine to end any relationships which are damaging and negative. Release the person with love, understanding you need healthy and positive people around you. Spend a day determined to be polite, even in the face of rudeness or adversity. Smile at strangers. Give the other guy a break; it can get you a break down the road.

Estelle Daniels

Honoring Your Deities and Protecting Your Home

In Hebrew mythology, the God of the Israelites sent the angel of death to Egypt, but he passed over any home visibly displaying allegiance to Him by placing lamb's blood on the doorpost. Magical people often guard the entryway to their homes with talismans, which can be designed to pay honor and tribute to a home's patron deities. Select the talisman's ingredients and shape by learning all you can about your patron deities and their sacred symbols. As you place the talisman on your doorpost, dedicate it to your deities by name, then say: "On this dwelling I place a charm, to ward away ill-will and harm; by the sacred blessings of three times three, as I will, so mote it be."

Edain McCoy

9 April

House Closing Spell

Before moving from a home, try this ritual. Take a wand and walk counter-clockwise around each room, twirling it counter-clockwise while visualizing all the good energy and memories of this place. Add some salt to a small bowl of water, saying, "I bless this representative of water with the representative of earth." Walk clockwise around each room, sprinkling the walls, windows, and doorframes with the water, while saying, "I cleanse this room with the elements of water and earth." Light some incense, and say, "I bless this representative of air with this representative of fire." Walk clockwise around each room while saying, "I cleanse this room with the elements of air and fire." When you get to your new home, walk clockwise around each room with the wand, visualizing all the happy memories unraveling into the new space.

Therese Francis

Aries Energy Spell

To tap into Aries energy, draw an image of an obstacle you are facing on a piece of paper. This can be a loose doodle or an accurate rendition. Then, on the back of the paper draw a representation of a desired outcome. On the bottom of the second drawing, write: "(Your name) using Mars energy (♂) focused through Aries energy (♈) overcomes the obstacle of (indicate difficulty)." At sunset present your petition to the spirit, asking for assistance in your current dilemma. Burn the drawing while watching the Sun dip below the horizon. As the fire of the heavens is absorbed into the horizon of the earth, the obstacle in your life will be absorbed by the universe and transmuted into positive energy. Mix the ashes with the petals of a red rose and scatter the mixture. Light a white candle, asking the spirit to bring purification into your life.

Silver RavenWolf

11 April

Travel Protection

To protect yourself during a driving trip, before departure walk clockwise around your car, and repeat the incantation: "As I travel near and far, I call on spirit to protect this car." On the front and back of the car draw the protection rune *(Eolh)* with your finger.

Sedwin

Tarot Spell for Successful Online Business Transactions

To promote successful online business transactions, during the waxing Moon place the Ace of Pentacles, Page of Wands, and Ace of Swords cards from your favorite tarot deck in a straight line on top of your CPU. Speak the following words: "An ace for money, a page for mail, an ace for victory—all of these I entreat." Then place one quartz crystal in your dominant hand, and chant: "A stone to magnify business success, and bring energy to my request." Place the stone on top of the Page of Rods card and say: "Busy my modem with commerce and trade; the spell commences as this stone is laid."

Dorothy Morrison

13 April

Getting Rid of Old Emotional Ties

To dissolve an obsolete emotional bond, when the Moon is waning or dark, strip naked and cast a circle. Light a thick incense such as dittany of Crete or Egyptian kyphi and swathe yourself in the smoke. As you do so, imagine the bond you wish to break protruding like an umbilical cord from your solar plexus. Now take saline solution and flick it all over the cord, envisaging it shedding white light as it absorbs into the emotional fibers of your old relationship. Witness the cord dissolving as you determine to lead a healthier emotional life. If the bond proves stubborn, produce an astral sword, and slice. When the bond is visibly broken, desist, cleansing your solar plexus with saline solution. As you do so, chant: "Hindrance out. Freshness in."

Kala Trobe

Stitch a Wish

To bring any positive wish you desire, take a sewing needle and red thread, a white handkerchief, a white candle, and your favorite incense. On the night of a Full Moon, as close to midnight as possible, light the candle and incense. Pass the handkerchief through the smoke of the incense, and think of your wish. Sew the thread through the handkerchief in any shape you desire, while saying: "With each stitch this spell I fix; with this thread the spell is fed. What I want will come to me; this is the way it must be!" Repeat the charm three times. Extinguish the candle and incense. Place the handkerchief beneath your pillow and expect a prophetic dream concerning your wish. Hide the handkerchief and repeat the spell in one lunar month if needed.

Jim Weaver

15 April

Protection Spell

Wearing elder *(Sambucus canadensis)*, either the white flowers or black berries, assists in warding off negative attacks. To expand protection to an entire household, hang the white flowers over the doorway to keep evil from crossing the threshold. If the vulnerability of sleep time disturbs you, place elder berries under the pillow before retiring to bed, and you will be free of nightmares.

Verna Gates

April 16

Spell to Bring Fairies to Your Garden

To bring fairies into your garden, plant rosemary or marigolds on the outer edges of your garden plot. Fairies like happy surroundings, so only work in the garden when you are feeling joyful or calm.

Therese Francis

17 April

Freezing Negativity Spell

The virtue of magic is often characterized by the nature of the practitioner. As long as there is a magical community, there will be people who use the magical arts for ill intent and for personal gain as well as those who strive to use the arts to improve the quality of life. Ideally, the first type of people would be retrained to use their skill for the benefit of all. However, at times, we may have to settle for merely stopping the hurt. To stop the negative actions of a misguided practitioner of magic, write his or her name on a piece of paper. Place the paper in a jar, and fill it with water. Place the jar in your freezer; as the water freezes, so will the ill actions of the negative practitioner.

Gwydion O'Hara

Computer Cleansing Spell

At times, you will read things or communicate with people via your computer and come away feeling angry or distraught. It is possible for negative energy to come through your computer just as spirits use a mirror as a portal. I've worked on the Internet long enough to know this. Therefore, I regularly take the time to remove the psychic build-up from my computer. To start, since computers don't like smoke or water I make a square pouch that will cover the computer screen, and I fill it with mugwort and sage, cedar, and lavender. Then I hang it over the screen of my monitor after I turn it off at night. This way, the herbs will absorb any negative energy. I refresh the herbs at least once a month.

Yasmine Galenorn

19 April

Almond Oil Blessing

Almond oil, the symbol of wakefulness to ancient Egyptians, is used in prosperity rituals and also added to money incenses. To make use of the powers of this oil, dip a ritual knife, candle, or piece of money into the oil, then raise the item to the sky and say:

> In the name of the Moon,
> Of the stars and of the Sun,
> I bless this oil.

Scott Cunningham

Irresistible Attraction Spell

To get attention when you're out where you might meet a new love, you will need some shiny body powder found at cosmetic counters and a lodestone or magnet. In a small glass vial mix the crushed powder with the lodestone while visualizing creating a powerful potion to draw positive attention and hold it there. Before you next go out in public, place an almost invisible layer of the powder on all visible parts of your body, including your hair if you like. This will create a reflective surface similar to the watch used by hypnotists to hold subjects' attention. Put the lodestone somewhere in your clothing and go out knowing all eyes will be drawn to you tonight.

Edain McCoy

Unwanted Habit Spell

To eliminate an unwanted habit or trait, make a puppet of yourself out of cloth, straw, or a carved candle. Make symbols or words on it to indicate what you want to release forever, allowing anger to build within you that you have practiced this unwanted behavior. Call upon Pluto or Hecate to assist your resolve to fully carry out change in your life. Then, using a safe container such as an iron cauldron or metal bowl, anoint the puppet with a few drops of oil of myrrh, pennyroyal, rosemary, or rue, and then carefully set it on fire, visualizing the release of your unwanted habit or trait forever. Burn the puppet to ashes, and then take the ashes to a place where you have no need to be at any time soon. Bury it, turn firmly, and walk away. Don't look back!

Maria Kay Simms

April 22

Earth Day

An Earth Day Blessing

Earth Day is designed to increase community awareness of important environmental issues and is dedicated to Mother Earth. As such, it is an appropriate time for Witches and Pagans throughout the world to perform Gaia-healing rituals. On this day, draw a pentagram on the ground using a sword, athame, wand, or your finger. Draw a circle clockwise around the pentagram and then place a new white candle in the center of the star. Light the candle, and as you gaze into its flames, focus your thoughts and energies upon the Earth, her rugged beauty and natural wonders, and recite: "Bless the Earth, bless the Earth. She is our mother, fertile and green. She is our healer. She is our queen. She is our teacher, ancient and wise. She must be cherished, let her not perish. She is our goddess in disguise."

Gerina Dunwich

23 April

Clay Moon Calendar Spell

Children are especially in tune with the Moon. This natural interest can be encouraged with a simple Moon project suitable for any age. First, create a ball of clay or dough to represent the Moon. Paint half of the Moon black and let it dry. Then, find a cap such as those used on vitamin bottles that you can use to hold the Moon. Determine the Moon phase for the day you will do this project, and arrange the crescent appropriately. For waxing Moons, the lit side will look like a "D." For waning Moons, the lit side will look like a "C." Each day, adjust the Moon to reflect its phase. You can simply use this to observe the Moon phases, or make a request on the dark of the Moon. Turn the Moon each day, and say these words, "Goddess of the Moon, you move so soon. Every day I wait, when will you grant my boon?" By the end of the Moon month, your request will be answered.

deTraci Regula

Spell for Self-Energizing

We all work hard these days and often find ourselves worn out as a result. To provide some self-energizing, this spell requires direct sunlight, either outdoors, or indoors at a south-facing window. Make yourself a tea that includes solar herbs such as cinnamon, cloves, orange, or lemon. (You may use citrus juice if you don't want something hot.) You will need some sort of solar stone, such as citrine or yellow tiger's-eye. Hold the stone up to the sunlight in your dominant hand, and hold the drink in your other hand. Say: "Helios Apollo, Sun-God, Healer, strengthen me with your light." Visualize the sunlight pouring into you, washing through you, especially your heart and solar plexus, and into both the drink and the stone. Drop the stone into the beverage; drink the beverage as quickly as is comfortable. Put the cup down and sit and soak up sunlight for as long as you can.

Martin Summerton

25 April

Car Protection Sachet

To make a magical sachet to protect you as you travel by car, mix two parts rosemary, two parts juniper, and one part each of mugwort, comfrey, and caraway. Add one small quartz crystal point, and tie everything up in a red cloth. Place the bundle somewhere in the car where it cannot be found, and drive safely. After a few months, take the sachet apart, save and cleanse the crystal, and use again in a new sachet.

Scott Cunningham

April 26

Spell for Financially Secure Progeny

If you're worried about your children's financial well-being, during a waxing Moon take ten new and shiny coins and place them in the pot of a flourishing plant. Then say this charm: "Be not earthed, pentacles bright, but grow and redouble in the palms of my children; multiply in the hands of my children's children." Visualize each of your offspring burgeoning like the plant itself. Next, place these coins in the palms of the three youngest members of the family, envisioning as you do a continual supply of gold passing into their lives. Be sure every year to channel some of your own lucre to your dependents to help fertilize their future.

Kala Trobe

27 April

New Love Tarot Spell

To attract new love, anoint a pink candle and
yourself with rose oil. Place a rose quartz in front
of the candle, and the Ace of Cups, the Page of
Cups, and the Lovers cards from your favorite
tarot deck left to right in front of the quartz. Following your breath, light the candle, saying, three
times: "Gentle love, come to me. Lift the veil so I
can see." Without visualizing a specific person,
imagine the soft, romantic, nurturing beginnings
of a new love. After fifteen minutes, extinguish
the candle and walk away. Begin on the first Friday of the New Moon and perform every night
until Full Moon, letting the candle burn all the
way down on the last day.

Cerridwen Iris Shea

Daily Card Spell

In addition to revealing complex patterns behind major events, tarot cards offer a way of examining the minute details of day-to-day life. For the latter purpose, you select a card for the day; most books recommend simply shuffling and then drawing one at random. Instead, try this: Cut the deck three times, reciting this charm as you do so: "Goddess of fortune, come what may—show me now the face of this day." Then shuffle the cards until one falls out of the deck, and use that as your card for the day. Look up its interpretation, which highlights the potential opportunities and challenges you will face. Pip (number) cards indicate minor or routine events, court (face) cards indicate important personal interactions, and trump (major arcana) cards indicate significant or unusual events. Keep a record of each day's card and events so you can track your accuracy.

Elizabeth Barrette

29 April

Spell for Feeling Overwhelmed

Every time you find yourself thinking, "I have too much to do," or "I don't have enough time," chant at least five times, "So much time, so little to do." You should feel better immediately.

Therese Francis

April 30

A Spell for Perfect California Poppies

California poppies are much more than just cheery flowers to brighten the garden. They bring the warmth and protective energy of their orange and gold color. To bring their magic to your property, plant some California poppies in the early spring, during the first or second phase of the Moon, when the Moon is in Virgo. Follow the package directions and place them in a sunny spot. After planting the seeds say: "Poppies, bright as the sun, your growth has now begun. Take root and take hold; bloom with flowers orange and gold." Give thanks to the Earth by pressing a penny into the seed bed; then water the seeds with a gentle spray of water. May you be blessed with a brilliant colony of California poppies.

Jim Weaver

1 May

Beltane Spell for Warding off Disease

Beltane is an appropriate time to perform spells to ward off disease, as the ancient Celts once drove their livestock through the smoke of their sacred Beltane bonfires to keep disease at bay. To perform this spell you will need a piece of white chalk and a white candle that has never before been burned. With the chalk, draw a pentagram on the floor about four feet wide. Light the white candle and hold it in your right hand. Step into the pentagram, face east, and thrice recite: "Beltane, fire of enchantment, burn without and within. Let this sabbat spell begin! Ofano, Oblamo, Ospergo, Hola Noa, Massa Lux Beff, Clemati, Adonai, Cleona, Florit, Pax Sax Sarax, Afa Afaca Nostra, Cerum Heaium, Lada Frium. So mote it be!"

Gerina Dunwich

Reserving a Good Parking Spot Spell

Just before you leave for a shopping trip or other short visit, call forth in your imagination a small familiar spirit or gremlin atop the hood of your car. Tell the creature "Hi!" in your mind. Call your little friend by a name of your choosing, and ask to have it locate and hold a good parking spot for you at your destination. Finish with "Now go!" As soon as you get to your destination and park in the space that has been held for you, be sure to call your friend forth onto your hood again, breathe five breaths of life force into your body, and direct it out to "bathe" your little friend in a shower of life energy.

Ed Fitch

3 May

Generating Luck Spell

Spells for generating luck are important, because they cover most of the good things we desire. One way to generate luck is to compile a "Book of Fortune." To begin, list your blessings in a blank book—striving to come up with 999 things that have been lucky for you. Even in an uneventful life, there are little serendipities—things found, recoveries made. Include emotional riches, such as each relationship you have enjoyed, memories of special occasions, and help you received from others. Also, write down your achievements and other good qualities. When you have counted 999 blessings, you can expect some special stroke of luck. However, your luck will increase well before that, because with every sentence you will be affirming the fact that you do have blessings. You can recite lines from this book as part of rites to strengthen your own spirit of luck.

Janina Renée

Taurus Energy Spell

To tap into Taurus energy, place the following in a
deep blue envelope: seven dried daisy petals, a
gold ribbon thirteen inches long with a knot tied
firmly around one iron nail on each end, and one
teaspoon of fertile earth. Seal the envelope with
gold wax imprinted with your fingerprint. On the
outside of the envelope draw the astrological
symbol of Venus (♍) and the symbol of Taurus
(♉). Hold your hands over the envelope and ask
the spirit to assist you in this situation. Be clear
about your intentions and needs. Seal the spell by
kissing the envelope. Bury the envelope in your
backyard. If you live in an apartment or condo-
minium, place the envelope at the bottom of a
flower pot and cover with potting soil.

Silver RavenWolf

5 May

Cinco de Mayo

The Magic Month of May

May is a time of year associated with other worlds. It was on May Eve that the Tuatha De Danann, the people of the goddess Danu and the forebearers of the fairies, arrived in Ireland. The fairy folk are at their most active during this month. Watch for fairy rings of toadstools or flowers. Leave an offering in the woods to make friends with them. May is also a good time to leave offerings at wells and springs, as the healing powers of water from sacred wells are amplified now. Take time now to get out-of-doors and re-new your connection with Mother Earth after the long dark winter. Regeneration of body and spirit is nurtured by warmer days and the resurgence of plant life. Get back into the garden (or start one) and let the Goddess reveal her cycles and wonder to you.

Sedwin

Anti-Insomnia Spell

Wrap handfuls of uncooked oats and dried camomile flowers, and a pinch of mandrake in a square of cheesecloth and filter a hot bath through it. Light some Egyptian kyphi incense and bathe while deeply breathing the aromas. In bed, envisage yourself in a field of camomile, like Dorothy surrounded by poppies in *The Wizard of Oz*. Think of lying down in the fragrant daisies, lulled to sleep by their fresh, sweet smell. Beneath the ground, the underworld; and above, in the blue sky, Witches and rainbow-hued elementals fly by on unimaginable missions. You lie drowsing in the fragrant flowers, following one of the passers-by, then another, tracing their patterns in the ether and following to the tunnel leading to the deep blue yonder.

Kala Trobe

7 May

Spell for Secrets

For a spell to help free you from your secrets, burn a black or dark red candle and meditate on the secrets you hold. Write down your secrets and imagine what might happen if they were revealed to the world. What are you hiding that is merely serving your ego? What are you hiding that protects yourself or others? What are you hiding because it gives you power? Tear the paper into small pieces and bury them in the earth if you want to keep those secrets, or flush them down the toilet if you want to eliminate them from your life.

Estelle Daniels

May 8

Lavender Bath

This spell will refresh and cleanse you. To begin, cast a circle in your bathroom. Call the elements, and light a lavender-colored candle. Then blend in a muslin bag a teaspoon each of lavender flowers, chamomile flowers, and dried crushed rosemary. Hang the sachet under the faucet, and draw your bath water, allowing it to pour down through the herbs. Add a half cup of lemon juice to the bath. When you settle into the tub, lean back, relax, and take three deep breaths. Close your eyes and focus on the excess tension and stress in your body. Feel the herbs and lemon draw it out of your muscles and mind. Thoroughly clean your tub when you are done to remove any residue of negative energy from the bath water.

Yasmine Galenorn

9 May

Moving Rituals

To smooth the transition when you move, you can perform a variety of rituals. When vacating the home, for instance, always leave some money behind, even if only a small amount. This will bring good luck to you as well as to your house's new tenants. Also, before moving into your new home, place a bit of dirt from your former property in your shoes. Leave it there until you have settled into your new place, and you will always have good times in your new home.

Scott Cunningham

Circle of Prosperity Spell

To make a circle of prosperity around your whole being, gather three thin bands: one of silver, one of gold, and one of copper. On the index finger of your left hand, place the gold band first, then the copper band, and finally the silver band. When you wish to have good fortune use them to call on Fortuna, goddess of good fortune. The best time to do this will be when the Sun is in Taurus.

Lori Bruno

11 May

The Daisy Love Spell

This spell will attract a virtuous lover, or bring honesty to your present relationship. First, obtain twenty-one bright yellow daisies, a water-filled vase, one pink candle, and some powdered coriander. Then, place the vase in front of you, and ask the water to bring a faithful lover to you. Focus on your intention throughout the ritual. Position the candle, symbolizing your lover, in front of the vase. Light it, and arrange seven daisies in the vase. Remove the petals from seven more daisies, and shower these around the vase and candle. Place the last seven daisies flat in front of you. Sprinkle the coriander over all the flowers. Finally, walk seven blocks from your home, and drop one daisy. Drop five more daisies on your way back. Leave the last daisy at your doorway, and expect a faithful love.

Marguerite Elsbeth

Calling Fairies Spell

Between Beltane and Midsummer's Eve, do this outdoors, preferably near water. Gather some St. John's Wort to guard against fairy mischief, and some food or milk. Cast a circle by sprinkling St. John's Wort on the ground around you. Stay within the circle, and repeat the following: "Goddess Dana, in whose name I sing, people of the hill and fairy ring—may your world be open to me. I come in peace—so mote it be." The ethereal fairies are as curious about us as we are of them. Enjoy their energy whether or not they reveal themselves. Leave a bit of food or milk to show your gratitude to them.

Sedwin

13 May

A Ritual to Honor the Mother Goddess

Place a white, female-shaped candle at the center of your altar, arranging fresh flowers around it. This candle represents the mother goddess; anoint it with three drops of frankincense and myrrh oil, and then light it with a match. After casting a circle and calling forth the guardians of the four elements, gaze into the flame of the candle, raise your arms in a traditional Witches' prayer position with palms turned up, and say: "Mother Goddess, creatress most ancient. This Witch's circle is consecrated to thee. You who are the giver of life; all that has been, all that is, and all that will be. This candlelight ritual I do perform in thy honor. You are the eternal and infinite queen of the gods and the greatest power on Earth, who commandest all that is. Praise be to thee, O Mother Goddess. So mote it be."

Gerina Dunwich

Dancing Broom Spell

This spell is helpful to cure the blues or just to get you moving on a sluggish day. Light a blue or white candle and some citrus-scented incense. Put your favorite up-tempo music on. Take your broom and start sweeping each room, first counterclockwise to remove any negativity, then clockwise to build harmony. When you feel like it, break into song and dance, taking the broom as your partner. Don't feel self-conscious—just enjoy!

Cerridwen Iris Shea

Spell to Banish Bad Vibes

If you just had a fight with your boyfriend or girl-friend, or your boss just chewed you out, this spell may help. As soon as you get home, take off all your clothes. Take a cleansing bath or shower. If you have a bathtub, put purifying herbs such as sage in the tub. Otherwise, light a stick of rose or sandalwood incense to burn while you shower, and pass the stick around you three times after you finish your shower. Then wash all the clothes you were wearing. If some of it has to be dry-cleaned, take it to the cleaners as soon as possible. Polish the shoes you were wearing if they are leather; otherwise, clean them off with a fresh rag. This will help clear any bad vibrations that may cling to you.

Magenta Griffith

Get-Your-Point-Across Spell

If you have been having trouble getting your point across, you may try this spell. Take one small piece of turquoise or turquoise jewelry and enchant the stone by saying: "Stone of sheer diplomacy, make my voice heard. The point that I must make today must not be disturbed. Remove the clouds, make clear the mark; as I will, so mote it be." Carry or wear the stone. This spell works especially well in difficult business meetings.

Dorothy Morrison

17 May

Breaking the Dam Spell

Assuming that something is "blocking" you from achieving success, here is a spell that can clear things up. To begin, walk along a body of water in some quiet, remote area. When you have found a shallow stream that feeds a little water into the main stream or the lake, think firmly of what is standing in the way of your life as you wade in and build a small dam to hold back the water. Continue building the dam wider and wider as the pool behind it gets bigger. When the dam eventually breaks or water begins cutting around the edge to bypass it, visualize your problem blockage area being cut away by the relentless powers of nature. Then, with a final "So mote it be," continue walking on down the beach.

Ed Fitch

Spell to Establish Stability in a Relationship

To establish some stability in an otherwise unstable relationship, light a brown or green candle and some juniper, frankincense, or neroli incense or oils. Picture yourself and your partner standing barefoot on grass, among green hills, embellishing as you deem fit. Maintain the image of your bare feet in contact with the earth, saying: "(Your lover's name), let no winds blow you away, let no fairy-lure tempt you, no charms ensnare you other than my own true love." Then, picture green shoots rising from the ground all around you, one of them becoming an ear of corn. Take the ear of corn and grind it to powder, saying: "Nurture what we have grown, that we may reap it together." Add to a cake, bread, or biscuit mix, and feed it to your lover. Repeat as necessary.

Kala Trobe

19 May

Tree Blessing Spell

Planting trees helps protect the environment and connect you to nature. You may use this spell to bless a new tree. First, plant a sapling in spring under a waxing or Full Moon using some organic fertilizer and a magical stone such as a quartz crystal or moss agate. While you work, repeat this chant: "Roots go down, grow deep and wide, anchor firmly side to side; trunk go up, grow tall and strong, keeping time to the seasons' song; leaves go out, thick and green, fair as any forest seen!" Put some fertilizer in the hole as you fill it, and sprinkle more on top. Set the stone by the trunk as a gift for the tree. Then cover everything with a layer of mulch. Thank the sapling for coming to live with you and promise to take care of it.

Elizabeth Barrette

A Yogurt Facial Spell

Yogurt is an ancient and magical food that is also beneficial to the skin. If you're having a hectic day, you can unwind with this spell. To start, you need a tablespoon of cold plain yogurt, a light blue candle, and gardenia incense. Light the candle and the incense; rinse your face with warm water and dry. As you pat on the yogurt, say this charm: "Wholesome food of the ancient ones, ease my tension. Nourish my spirit and my skin; make me fresh again. Blessed be!" Kick back and relax or soak in the tub. Leave the yogurt on your face for about ten minutes. Rinse with cool water and pat dry. You'll be refreshed. Tip: This spell also works well for a mild case of sunburn.

Jim Weaver

21 May

Cat Divination for Fortune

When you drive off to work in the morning, do a "cat count" on the way out of your neighborhood. Look for cats resting peacefully on porches or fences, under bushes or parked cars. The more cats you find enjoying the light of the new morning, the more likely you will find good fortune in the coming day!

Ed Fitch

Spell Against Spells

Feeling embattled at work? Gather together five pens or pencils. Hold them between your hands and call on your patron deity to witness your spell, saying, "These pens are mightier than swords and stronger than wands. They protect and defend me in my work." Determine the direction the trouble comes from, and lay the pens in front of you. Angle the first pen so it tilts up from left to right, the second so it tilts down from right to left, forming two sides of a triangle. Balance the third pen sweeping up at an angle from lower right to upper left. The fourth pen forms the crossbar, and the fifth pen brings this banishing pentagram together. Hint: If the pens won't stay in place easily, wrap a rubber band around one end of each pen. Leave in place till the end of the day or until you feel the problem is passing.

deTraci Regula

23 May

Luggage Protection Charm

Though this may at times seem a futile endeavor, you may make a charm to protect your luggage on a long trip. To begin, in a white muslin bag place two teaspoons each of rosemary, chamomile, frankincense, and lavender, and a piece of dragon's blood resin. Add a silver dime, a piece of quartz crystal, and a polished piece of tiger's-eye. Tie the bag shut and focus energy into it, visualizing the sachet emanating a protective energy that surrounds your luggage, keeping it safe from thieves and from being lost. Make a sachet for each piece of your luggage and tuck it into the contents.

Yasmine Galenorn

# May 24

To Ensure Success in Business Proposals

To ensure success in any business proposal, lick your finger and use it to draw a pentacle on the back of each sheet of the proposal packet. Place the proposal in an envelope and draw a pentacle on its back as well, while chanting: "With spit of tongue, stout magic mesh with these sheets; bring success to me. So mote it be!" Contracts usually come within a two-week period. This spell is especially helpful when Mercury is retrograde.

Dorothy Morrison

25 May

Morning Dew Spell

The dew in May has always been the Witch's beauty secret. An old Cornish proverb associated with the May solar festival of Beltane says: "The fair maid who, on the first of May, goes to the fields at break of day, and bathes in dew from the hawthorn tree, will ever strong and handsome be." During a waxing Moon, take a small bowl outdoors and place on the grass. Anoint the rim with vanilla or ginseng and make a statement of your desire to enhance your looks. The next day, use your hands to bathe your face in the collected dew. Bathe other visible parts of your body with any remaining water. Be sure to visualize clearly the outcome you desire as often as you can from the time you first touch the bowl until the spell is done.

Edain McCoy

Seed Choosing Divination

Deciding on the seeds to cultivate in your garden is challenging, since there are so many wonderful varieties to choose from. This simple divination can help you make up your mind. First, decide how many of each type—such as corn, beans, and herbs—you have room for. Then, list candidates—such as silver queen corn or kandy korn—suitable for your area. Write down their names on separate slips of paper or cut out the catalog entries. Then make this invocation to Demeter: "Green mother, I beseech you: Share with me your bounty and show me which seeds to plant so they grow strong!" Take all the slips for one type of crop and toss them in the air. Remove the ones that fall face-down, and repeat as necessary until you have as many face-up slips remaining as you have room to plant. The face-up slips indicate your best choices. Thank Demeter and make your order.

Elizabeth Barrette

27 May

Self-Healing Spell

For self-healing in general, and for a head cold in particular, mix eucalyptus leaves, peppermint, thyme, and rose petals in Epsom salts and wrap in cheesecloth. Tie up the ends tightly with cord or ribbon, and wrap yourself in a warm robe. Light a candle in an aromatherapy burner with a little water and several drops of eucalyptus oil in the top. Place it very near your bathtub. Draw a steaming bath, hotter than you can immediately enter. Call upon the goddesses of the sea—Mary, Yemaya, Isis—to heal you, and toss the cheese-cloth sachet into the hot water. Inhale the eucalyptus oil scent deeply. Test the water, disrobe, and ease yourself in. Soak in the steam and relax. Run more hot water as needed. After your bath, wrap up warmly again, add oil to your aromatherapy burner and continue to inhale the eucalyptus-scented moist air as you rest.

Maria Kay Simms

Spell to Attract Friendly Garden Spirits

Gazing globes were originally used as a tool to protect property from the evil stares of passersby. Garden spirits also love them and are attracted by their shiny surfaces. To charge a gazing globe so it will attract a friendly garden spirit, during a spring or summer Full Moon wash your globe with bottled spring water. Place it in your garden and say: "Gazing globe round as Moon, protect each plant and bloom. With your reflective light, attract fairy and sprite." Then, in the garden near the globe, place an oak leaf, a sprig of ivy, and a fern leaf. Garden spirits will know they are now welcome in your garden. Show your thanks occasionally by leaving a shiny new penny or a sprinkle of bird seed.

Jim Weaver

29 May

Purification Spell for Earth

This little incantation has a variety of uses, especially for the magical person who's constantly on the go. You can repeat this in a subway station, while relaxing in the park, when walking down a dark street at night, or when entering an unfamiliar place that makes you feel nervous: "Earth to earth, angels to ancestors. Riches to riches, treasure to treasure. Heath to hearth, bring blessings of the mother upon me, Earth." To add extra pizzazz to your magical work, carve the zodiac symbols that relate to the earth (Taurus, Virgo, Capricorn) on the candle color of your choice, or mix up an earth powder that includes soil, salt, and a variety of herbs and place all in a conjuring bag.

Silver RavenWolf

Computer Maintenance Spells

Computer users know you should do weekly backups of important files. Also, a good time to go through and delete unnecessary files, and to defragment the hard drive, is late during the waning Moon. This is an especially good time for these activities. If you have a Mac, you need to re-install the operating system regularly. This is best done during a waxing Moon.

Martin Summerton

31 May

Meteor Spell

On the night of a meteor shower, go far from the city lights and find a comfortable and warm place to look up at the sky. As you watch, hum a tune that, to you, has a particularly magical feel to it, and build up a firm picture in your mind of the things you truly and sincerely desire. Then, when you see a shooting star, send forth your wish for prosperity or success or any other thing on the star.

Ed Fitch

June 1

The Flowering Footprint Love Spell

I hope your lover leaves a good footprint impression in the dirt, for this love spell works on your lover through the earth upon which he or she walks. To start, follow your lover's footsteps without being seen. Wait until your lover is out of sight, and dig up the footprint along with the surrounding earth. Put it in a plastic bag and bring it home. Now, carve your lover's name on the side of a clay flower pot, and place the earth inside. Plant marigolds, symbolizing everlasting love, and bury a rose quartz crystal in the pot. As the golden blossoms grow and bloom and never fade, so will your sweetheart's love for you do the same. Enhance this spell by shredding a few of the marigold blossoms into your favorite salad. See your lover walking in your direction as you dine.

Marguerite Elsbeth

2 June

Whispering Wind Spell

This is a spell to assist if something is bothering you or if you have a strong, unfulfilled desire. To begin, make sure there is a slight breeze blowing. Light a yellow jar candle and take a few minutes to meditate on your desire or problem. Open the window and whisper your problem or desire, asking the angel of the east to hear and respond. Let the wind carry your words to the east. Burn the candle down whenever you are home until it is burned out. An answer should come to you within one Moon cycle.

Cerridwen Iris Shea

Revitalization Meditation

Occasionally the wheel of the world gets a little stuck. This spell gives it a nudge when you feel overwhelmed by challenges. To start, do something nice for a person needier than you; this can be as simple as shopping for a housebound friend or as complex as cleaning your closet to donate clothes to charity. Next, take a milk bath, a traditional way to nourish body and soul: Pour a can of condensed milk into your bathwater and soak for at least ten minutes. Meditate on the infinite abundance of the universe and visualize it flowing your way. Recite this mantra as you soak: "With open hands and open heart—as I have given, I receive—love and hope and miracles, and the power to believe." Finish with an invigorating shower. Over the next days, whenever you need reassurance or courage, repeat the mantra. Help is on the way!

Elizabeth Barrette

4 June

Group Table Blessing

To bless the food at a table, have each person in the dinner party say a part of this blessing to the bounty embodied in the God and Goddess union.

> All fruits of the Earth
> are fruits of your union.
> Your womb, your dance,
> Lady and Lord.
> Come, join with us,
> Feast with us,
> Enjoy with us!

Therese Francis

Spell for Other Cultures

For a spell to help you understand other cultures, eat at a foreign restaurant and think about how a cuisine reflects the culture it comes from. Light a purple candle and think about any prejudices you might hold—we all have them. Write down your prejudices. As the candle burns, release any hatred and ill feelings and try to envision yourself understanding other people, even those from different backgrounds and cultures. Envision yourself building a bridge of understanding between yourself and one other person with whom you have little in common. Burn the paper and let go of one prejudice.

Estelle Daniels

6 June

Gemini Energy Spell

You can use this magical Mercury powder by it-self, or add the powder to other forms of magic—such as at the bottom of a candle or in a cauldron—to find information and encourage communications. To start, grind and mix the fol-lowing ingredients with a mortar and pestle: dried white rose petals, silver glitter, blue powder, dried vervain, and dried orris root. With your finger or a pencil, draw the symbol of Mercury (☿) and the symbol of Gemini (♊) in the powder. Hold your hands over the powder, asking that the mixture be instilled with the dynamic energies of Gemini. Store the powder in a plastic bag that contains a moonstone. To put to use, place a teaspoon of the Mercury powder in the palm of your hand and blow off your fingers as you ask the element of air to speed your request and return the necessary details to you as quickly as possible.

Silver RavenWolf

Spell to Increase Cash Flow

To increase your business cash flow, hold a piece of adventurine in your dominant hand during the waxing Moon. Concentrate on money flowing into your business, and cast an enchantment through the stone by saying: "Money come, money grow; increase my money flow. Fill my cash box to the top; then may it never stop." Place the stone in your cash register or bank bag.

Dorothy Morrison

8 June

Keeping Your Lover

To prevent the loss of your lover, during the waxing Moon take a lock of your partner's hair and plait or mix it with your own, contemplating your essences intermingling. Wrap the hair along with a personal artifact from each person in a red silk square, and bind with a ribbon of green, chanting: "Love to the left of us, love to the right of us, over us, under us, ever uniting us." Envision the red silk as your mutual love, the ribbon as your spellbinding. Tie it tight. Attach a sprig of berried holly to the center of the package, saying: "Prickles defend our love." Place the bundle in a black star-spangled box. Do not open or untie unless you wish to break the bond.

Kala Trobe

Saturn Reorganizes Spell

After you spend a day cleaning and organizing, try this meditation, which utilizes Saturnian colors to welcome good things to your home. Use black in the home office to help you meditate on keeping good finances—money in the bank, bills paid. Black absorbs all and attracts prosperity. Use brown in the living room—wood furniture gleaming with lemon oil, bookshelves full of wonders. The wood is warm and inviting. Use red in the kitchen as a symbol of nourishment and health; visualize a big stew pot on a glowing red burner. Visualize salsa, red peppers, pasta sauces, and so on. Use indigo in the bedroom to help you visualize the night sky dotted with stars. Indigo calms, welcomes sleep, encourages rest; it feels peaceful here.

Denise Dumars

10 June

General Good Health and Abundance Spell

To promote general good health and abundance in your life, squeeze a lemon into one cup of water while thinking of all the good things you want to flow into your life. Hold the cup of lemon water while humming a perfect pitch A (440 cycles per second) note for one minute. Then drink the water and lemon mixture.

Therese Francis

Moon Soak Spell

To relax and become attuned with the Goddess at the end of your busy day, treat yourself to a Moon soak. To start, prepare a small dish of white flower petals mixed lightly with Epsom salts and scented with a few drops of jasmine oil. Have ready a silver or a light blue candle and draw a warm bath. Light your candle and turn off all other lights, adding some soft background music if you so choose. Disrobe and look out a window, if possible, to see the Moon. If you can't see her, visualize her in whatever phase she is in. Ask the Lady of the Moon to bless you, and draw down her power, as you anoint your forehead, head, throat, heart, abdomen, loins, and feet, each with a drop of jasmine oil. Now, toss your Epsom salt mixture into the bath, step in, and enjoy.

Maria Kay Simms

12 June

Sacred Space Purification Spell

To purify a sacred space, during the sixth hour after sunrise or the first or eighth hour after sunset consecrate an aromatherapy bowl or small cooking pot by passing it through the smoke of frankincense and sprinkling it with blessed water, saying: "I consecrate this container to aid in my Craft, that the spell I now weave will take hold and last." Heat spring water in the bowl over a tea light or in the pot on a burner. When the water is hot, add the following herbs, speaking after each—star anise: "Let all negativity be deflected from this place"; one bay leaf: "As the scent of this leaf moves through this place, may purification enter into this space"; one teaspoon sage: "Through sage I now make this spell manifest, that with peace and protection this space will be blessed. For as I will, so mote it be!"

Ann Moura

June 13

Safety Map Spell

To ensure safety before taking a long trip, get out a map of the area through which you are going to be traveling. Cast a circle, and then, using a green pen, trace the route you're going to take. After you've done so, take a piece of white chalk and lightly color over the entire itinerary with a thin layer, visualizing the white chalk as a glowing light of protection along the route. Then, place a row of amethyst or tiger's-eye, or a string of beads, along the route and say: "Guard and guide our trip, and all who venture on this road. See us safely to our destination, see us safely home. Blessed be." Visualize yourself arriving safely. Fold the map, with the crystals inside, and tie it with a white ribbon. Keep it on your altar or in a safe place until you return.

Yasmine Galenorn

14 June

Basil Business Spell

Basil is well-known as a money-drawing herb. Here's a spell you can do on your lunch hour to bring money your way. To start, go to a Thai restaurant and order a dish that includes basil, hot chilis, and, ideally, coconut milk. There should be at least one such dish on any Thai menu. Order this dish during business lunches, or bring it back to work to eat in the lunchroom. If you own a business, let the scent of the basil dish waft through your workplace. Say aloud or to yourself: "Oh Basilia, goddess of plenty, your rich green leaves bring us prosperity, health, and love. Help our business grow and prosper." Then, as a gesture to Basilia, buy a basil plant the next time you visit a garden shop. Keep it at work and keep it watered and healthy. Your business should thrive.

Denise Dumars

Lifting Shyness Spell

You know the story—he's cute, but doesn't seem to have much to say. This spell is for use when an available person seems interested but reticent. To start, take a small key, hold it to your bosom and say: "Confident be he who holds this key, that my treasures will yielded be." Blast the key with vibrant, come-hither energy; then embalm the symbol in rosemary oil, saying: "Hesitate not, future lover, but your feelings now uncover." Pass the key several times through the smoke of some fragrant incense, and say: "Inhibitions float away, love and lust are here to stay." Send the key one last bolt of Venusian allure, and slip it into your potential lover's pocket or bag. Let him work the rest out for himself. (This spell works when your future lover is a woman, too.)

Kala Trobe

16 June

Tree Talking

For this spell, go barefoot into a forest with a container of water. Find a tree that seems, for some reason, to have a particular strength to it—perhaps from age or character. Greet the tree, and pouring the water about its base, state your wish to talk with it. Find what seems to you to be the proper location around the tree, plant your feet firmly, hold onto the tree as you press yourself against it. Dig your toes strongly into the ground, imagining that you are sending forth your own roots into the earth. Close your eyes and press your forehead against the bark of the tree. "Speak" to the tree in images and feelings, and leave your mind open to feel what the tree is feeling. Feel the life-force as it flows within the trunk of your tree-friend, and understand the tree's outlook on existence. Take your time. Experience, and enjoy yourself.

Ed Fitch

Lost Manhood Spell

To perform a spell to restore lost manhood, you will need two old iron keys, some musk oil, three crimson red candles, musk, jasmine or vanilla incense, and a handful of red rose petals. Before making love, anoint each key with three drops of musk oil and then place them beneath the mattress in the form of an X. Arrange the candles on the floor—one at each side of the bed and one at the foot of the bed. Anoint each with three drops of the oil, and then light the candles and incense to infuse the bedroom with sensual vibrations. Relax, fill your mind with erotic thoughts, and recite the following incantation: "With keys of iron, oiled and crossed, be restored my manhood! Fire of virility, storm of passion—now I raise thee!"

Gerina Dunwich

18 June

A Blessing for a New Home

To give your new home a psychic cleansing, try this spell. Take a new broom and lightly anoint the tips of the bristles with a teaspoon or so of crushed almonds (for happiness) combined with a drop or two of honey (for the sweetness of life). Then at sunrise (never sunset), sweep your front porch or main threshold with your anointed broom. Visualize sweeping away all negative energy as you say this charm: "With this broom I sweep away all negativity, till only peace and calm surround me. As I destroy all discord, I sweep in harmony and accord." Use this spell anytime you feel a need to cleanse your home, or after a grouch has darkened your doorway!

Jim Weaver

Create a Cleansing Altar

To create an altar for use in cleansing cere-
monies, first cover a small table with a white
cloth, preferably linen. Arrange on the cloth one
freshly cleansed amethyst crystal, a thriving fern
plant, a smudge stick in a small bowl of salt, a
crystal candle holder with a white or lavender
candle, and a bowl of dried lavender, rosemary,
chamomile, and dill. Light the smudge stick and
blow the incense around the altar, saying: "Spirits
of protection, healing, and cleansing, bless the objects on this altar—that I might use them to aid
in cleansing and purifying during my magical
work. Blessed be." Whenever you have need,
come to the altar and work your cleansing, purifying, and healing magic here. You may place pictures on the amethyst and ask that the person or
object in the photograph be cleansed as well.

Yasmine Galenorn

20 June

Almost-Out-of-Gas Spell

If you are traveling by car and low on fuel, but are far from the nearest gas station, here is a spell that may help. First, relax. Even if you do run out of gas, it will not be a disaster, because a friendly motorist would help you. Second, remind yourself that you won't run out of gas, because there is a reserve in the tank even when it reads "empty," and because this magic spell is protecting you. Third, center yourself and enter an alert state of mind. Fourth, take a deep breath. As you exhale, imagine your breath flowing under the car and lifting it just a bit so the engine works more easily. Fifth, focus on your driving. Notice how effortlessly the car moves, floating over the road. When you look at the gauge, you will notice the car has used almost no gas in the last several miles.

Amber K

June 21

Solstice Spell

In parts of Egypt, before the building of the Aswan dam, the Solstice marked the beginning of the Nile flooding, which brought abundance to the Nile Valley. To tap into this magic, take twelve coins from your pocket, one for each month of the year, and at a table pile them as far away from you as possible. One by one, move three of the coins toward you and let them fall into your lap, saying: "The flood begins." Move another three to you, saying: "The water is rising." Move the third set of three to you, saying: "The flood is adequate this year." Finally, move the last three coins to you, announcing with conviction: "This year is abundant; all will thrive with this year's flood!" Keep the twelve coins in a small bowl until next Solstice. Draw one out each month so that you always know you have money coming to you.

deTraci Regula

22 June

A Talisman for Love

To make a talisman to draw new love into your life you will need a Moon-drenched night, preferably during a Full Moon, and a needle and thread and some pink or red felt. Sew the felt into a small pouch, and place items magically charged to draw love—love letters, your nail clippings, song lyrics, and love herbs such as vanilla, rue, myrtle, violet, rose, apricot, apple, yarrow, rosemary, thyme, meadowsweet, lemon, dragon's blood, clove, or dill. A rose or clear quartz crystal may also be added. Sew up the pouch while the light of the Moon washes over it and say: "By my hands the spell is begun; love comes to me through what I have done." Rededicate the talisman at each Full Moon and carry it with you until you find the love you seek.

Edain McCoy

Runic Naming Spell

Many people like to give names to important objects such as their altar tools, their cars, and their computers. Sometimes the right name just pops into your mind, but other times you need a little help. This spell uses rune dice to suggest a secret magical name and a public everyday name for a new object. Begin by placing a piece of cloth on or near the object you wish to name. Select one of the rune dice at random and toss it onto the cloth. The facedown symbol indicates the secret name and nature of your object, while the faceup symbol indicates the public ones. Look up the associations in a rune book and meditate on the meaning of these runes; then use red ink or paint to mark the runes on the object to be named.

Elizabeth Barrette

24 June

Deep Sleep Spell

To ensure a deep sleep, fill the sink with warm water before going to bed every night. Add five to ten drops of lavender oil, and splash the water on your face, the back of your neck, your wrists, elbows, stomach, knees, and ankles. Alternatively, you may shower and then take a hot soaking bath in a lavender tea. To make the tea, boil a quart of water. Remove from heat and add a half-cup lavender flowers. Steep for five minutes; then strain. Pour the lavender tea into a tub filled with hot water and enjoy.

Therese Francis

Energy and Resolve Spell

Some of us, upon returning home from work, school, travel, or other tiresome activities, have an immediate urge to collapse into a chair to watch TV and vegetate. Unfortunately, this means that we avoid other more important activities, such as our house work and chores. To train your energy after a long day, keep in your glove compartment a necklace or pouch of stones such as jasper, tiger's-eye, carnelian, or other objects that promote energy and efficiency. Before starting the drive home, handle the stones and visualize yourself arriving home and spending ten minutes tidying something (in one seamless motion) before you relax. Recall this visualization as you drive. If you are able to stick to this discipline, you can gradually increase the amount of time you spend cleaning.

Janina Renée

26 June

Magical Strength Spell

To build your own magical strength, stand out in
the open on a dark moonless night. Then, pick out
a star directly overhead and gaze steadily at it.
With your mind, will it to move first to one way
and then to another. It will.

Ed Fitch

June 27

A Spell to Reduce Defensiveness in Communications

If you encounter someone who seems very closed and defensive, unwilling or unable to hear what you have to say, try this spell. Sit down or place yourself lower than the other person. Be loose and relaxed; do not cross your arms or legs. Make your breathing slow and even. Visualize your aura (energy field) and draw it close to you. Imagine yourself holding a sword, and the other party holding a huge shield. Between you is a stone wall. In your mind's eye, put down the sword and watch the wall fade away. Silently invite your opposite to set aside the shield. Now invite the other party to speak, by saying something such as, "Can you tell me how you're feeling right now?" Listen, and listen some more. Watch the other's defenses melt.

Amber K

28 June

Juno's Day

Juno is the great organizer of society, and she rules city hall, courthouses, lawyer's offices, and banks—you may even find a likeness of her on a public building. She deserves a rightful place alongside Thor and Jupiter. It is probably no accident that there is an e-mail provider called Juno, as she works well with technology issues, too. You may choose to call upon Juno if you have legal, civic, or banking issues to deal with today, or if your computer is acting up. Try wearing a mix of patchouli oil with a not-too-sweet feminine scent like neroli, lavender, or melissa. Wear royal purple or orange, the color of intellect. Season food with a bay leaf to release the power of bay laurel. Imagine Juno as your protector as you conduct your business.

Denise Dumars

Cat Spell

According to a French superstition, you don't see many cats on Friday because they go to Finisterre to report to the Devil after spending the week spying on human families. (Finisterre is the westernmost region of Brittany, a place with strong ties to a Celtic past.) Because such negative beliefs are often inversions of old traditions resulting from the Church's attempt to put down the old religions, this may be a survival of a Pagan belief that the cats go to Finisterre to dance with the fairies. Therefore, Witches can use this belief as an opportunity to strengthen a relationship with the fairy realm. Tie a red string, loosely, around your cat's neck, reciting: "Whither you wander, you carry my blessings." If the cat comes home without it, you'll know the fairy folk accept and return your good wishes.

Janina Renée

30 June

Ocean Energy Meditation

If you live near an ocean, try this meditation designed to increase energy while promoting relaxation. Stand at the edge of the ocean and inhale its scent; listen to the waves as you gaze at the sea. When a wave comes in, scoop some water: Feel it; taste it. Breathe in as a wave recedes, breathe out as a wave breaks. Shrug your shoulders a few times. Close your eyes again and meditate on an ocean deity or spirit such as Yemaya, Tiamat, Neptune, Poseidon, Isis Pelagia, or Aphrodite. Feel the tension flow from your neck and shoulders, flowing down to the sand. Now open your eyes. Symbolically hug the ocean to your breast. Feel the power of the waves; absorb energy from the ocean. Feel your energy level rise. Thank the ocean for its blessings, and bless it in return. Now have a great day!

Denise Dumars

Getting Rid of Warts Spell

To get rid of an unwanted wart, cover it with a piece of fresh banana peel and tape in place. Imagine the virus being washed away by running water. Hold this meditation for five minutes, then leave the taped banana peel in place. Replace the banana peel twice a day for five days. Do the meditation whenever you think of it. The area will look blistery when you change the banana peel the first few days; that means this spell is working.

Therese Francis

2 July

Cancer Energy Spell

To encourage the rebuilding of something, or to promote protection, at night gather one bowl of water, three jade stones, and thirteen new dimes. Empower the bowl of water under the Full Moon by capturing the reflection of the Moon in the water for at least thirty minutes. Slowly drop each dime in the water, waiting until the water stills before you drop each one. Make your intention known as you use all the dimes. Then, hold your hands over the bowl and repeat your request. In the air, over the bowl, draw the sigil for the Moon (☽) and the sigil for Cancer (♋). Take the three stones and the thirteen dimes and place them in a green conjuring bag. Sprinkle the water at the threshold of all doors leading to the outside, repeating your petition. Keep the bag with you until your request is answered.

Silver RavenWolf

Kitchen Witch Purification Spell

No time to cast a circle and perform a long purification ritual? No problem! Into a large enamel saucepan, add two minced large onions, five minced cloves of garlic, two tablespoons dried rosemary, two sliced lemons, and two tablespoons of crushed black peppercorns. Cover with three quarts of water and bring to a rolling boil. Let the steam permeate the house; carry the pan carefully through the house into each room so that the steam can filter into every nook and cranny. When this is finished, open the windows and let the wind blow through to take away the last remnants of day-to-day tension and stress.

Yasmine Galenorn

4 July

Empathy Spell

When communication with someone founders, you can sometimes understand what is happening by using the empathy spell. First, chant silently to yourself: "Me in thee, what do I see?" Then imagine yourself in the other person's shoes, talking to you. Ask your new self these questions: "How do I feel? What do I want? Why do I want it? How can I get it? What do I fear? How do I see the other party in this conversation (your old self)? As friend? Potential ally? Obstacle? Enemy? A vague person? What am I seeing that the other party isn't seeing?" Then return to your own skin and check your new understanding by asking some careful neutral questions, such as, "If I'm understanding correctly, this is what you want. True?" Once you understand the other party, you will quickly know whether agreement is possible and what it will take to achieve it.

Amber K

Spell for Getting Organized

To utilize "getting organized" energies, light a brown, dark blue, or black candle, and think about your life: where you are, where you have come from, the choices you have made, and the opportunities you have taken or missed. How does all this mesh with what you envisioned for yourself when you were younger? Are you following in your family's footsteps, or have you gone off in your own direction? Where do you want to be? Write all this down, and when you are done burn the paper releasing your ambitions to the cosmos. Concentrate on your work and how it benefits society.

Estelle Daniels

6 July

Italian Passion Spell

Use this spell to affect someone who desires you, yet is shy in expressing his or her feelings. Start by melting some red candle wax and molding it in the shape of a phallus if you are female, or a womb if you are male. Once the wax has dried, sensuously anoint the candle with olive oil, as if you were attending your lover, thinking hard on the intimacy you desire as you do so. Light the candle. Now, write your lover's name three times on a piece of white paper, and burn it in the flaming wick, praying that your lover will come to you. While the paper burns, recite your lover's name out loud three times, then blow out the candle. Try to wait patiently for your lover to respond to your magic.

Marguerite Elsbeth

Wish Upon the Moon Spell

To request a wish, inscribe the symbol of the waxing Moon in a pure beeswax candle with a rose thorn. Light the candle, and with your eyes focused upon the flame concentrate on your wish. When the wish is firmly in your thoughts, chant: "Gracious Lady Moon, mother of love and light, grant my wish. Fulfill my dreams. Smile on me tonight." Extinguish the candle flame, but hold its memory in your mind for as long as you can. As you dwell upon the vision of the burning flame, know that your request has been heard. Within the space of a lunar cycle, your wish should be granted.

Gwydion O'Hara

8 July

Get Pregnant Spell

If you are hoping to get pregnant, set aside several hours with your partner when the Moon is full in a water sign—Cancer, Scorpio, or Pisces. Light a white candle and, together, clearly state that you wish to parent a child. Tell each other what your dreams are for this child, and how this child will change your lives. Be realistic and honest with each other. As one white candle burns out, light another; then demonstrate the level of care that you will provide for the child by showing care for each other. You may do this through anything sensual, such as massage, bathing, or snuggling. After the sex act, continue showing care for each other for at least another hour. During this time, restate that your intent is to bring a child into your family, and that you will show the child the same level of care that you are currently showing to each other.

Therese Francis

Spell to Establish Concord Between Rival Siblings

Had the nine Muses fought the way most sisters do, humanity's arts would be much the poorer. To help establish sibling harmony among your children, bind objects symbolic of each child with a six-foot-long brown ribbon. As you do so, repeat: "Binah brought you unto me. Mother goddess, hear this plea. Let my children happy be; bound in soulful harmony." If the Moon is waxing, you should contemplate a growth of love among the siblings; if waning, meditate on diminishing hostility. Pull the ribbon tight, and knot. Every time they fight, think of their goddess-blessed unity. It will not take long for the spell to take practical effect.

Kala Trobe

10 July

Purification Spell for Water

The incantation below is a purification spell that you can use as part of a larger working, or alone when swimming, walking in the rain, boating, and so on. It can also be used in preparing for the birth of a baby, or during the birthing process. If necessary, use the incantation as a drought-buster. Begin by saying: "Water protects the embryo, ancestor love of long ago. Tides and rivers dance and flow, enchant this place, let magic grow. Revive! Bring change! I make it so." For added water energy in magic, carve the zodiac symbols of Cancer, Pisces, and Scorpio on the candle color of your choice, and stand the candle in one-half inch of water as it burns.

Silver RavenWolf

Effective Communication Bath

If you are looking to increase your communication skills, you may choose to cast this bathing spell during the waning Moon. Toss a handful of table salt and a single black onyx into your bath water and chant: "Wash all mental blocks with this stone. All negativity, all that has hold on me, banished be; my thoughts flow clear and free." Immerse yourself in the bath completely nine times. Allow your body to dry naturally; then bury the stone or release it into a body of water.

Dorothy Morrison

12 July

Spell for Women in Public Service

Juno can be a powerful ally to women in government and public service jobs. This spell can be used to help your elected representatives, or to elect more women to public offices, and to strengthen women's influence in public life. Wear cypress oil, your best business attire, and moonstone or silver jewelry. Close your eyes; ground and center, and envision your elected representative in a royal purple or electric blue suit. See her succeeding, whether it's at speaking before Congress or the library board. Now transform her into Juno, a regal matron in a Roman toga with purple sash. She blesses the audience with a silver wand and fills the scene with cool moonfire, the fire of reason and compassion. Repeat for each woman you wish to help. Thank Juno and relax. Repeat monthly to bolster women's public roles.

Denise Dumars

Sexual Attraction Spell

To increase sexual attraction, cast this spell when the Moon is waxing, and during the season at or near Beltane or the start of Lammas. To begin, girdle your thigh with a green garter. Become an Aphrodite (entranced by thoughts of love) as you place this erotic symbol about your limb, and light a pink or green candle in honor of the beauteous goddess, saying: "Venus, Astarte, Inanna, Ishtar, may your power be compounded in this garter I wear." Imagine the ancient impetus to merge and procreate summarized on your thigh, spreading its irresistible aura about your person. Now say: "Let only those I choose perceive this charm." After all, you do not want every Tom, Dick, and Harriet harassing you. Concentrate until you feel your allure. Establish your magnetism with a confident smile.

Kala Trobe

14 July

Crystal Charge Spell

This is an all-purpose spell for charging your magic crystals and stones. To start, collect the crystals and stones that you use in ritual or simply keep in your house because they have attracted you. Just before a Full Moon, cleanse them with salt water, then place on a windowsill where the light of the Full Moon can bathe them. A night or two after the Full Moon, place the crystals and stones in a circle on the floor as you cast a circle. Sit in the center of the circle and let the energy of the crystals and stones come into you. Softly chant: "Crystal vision, crystal sight, let me find my power this night." You may want to come prepared with a question or issue you'd like to resolve. Clear your mind and let the answer flow in. When it feels appropriate, ground your energy and thank the crystals and stones for their help.

Sedwin

Sun Blessing Spell

This is a day for extending blessings, as the Sun's rays bless the Earth on this day. Spreading blessings was also one of the customs of the legendary fey, and it is something that you can do to extend your power outward. As an ongoing blessing spell, cut small bird shapes out of construction paper in your idle moments, and thread string through them so they can be hung. Write a cheerful word of blessing such as "hope," "love," or "luck" on each bird. If you wish, embellish each one by drawing details or gluing glitter on them. Then, whenever you go out—whether to walk in a park, visit a friend's house, shop at the mall, and so on—surreptitiously hang a string of birds in bushes or other secretive places. Know that your birds are acting as agents of your power, blessing any person who comes across them.

Janina Renée

16 July

Cat Communication Spell

If you have been having trouble communicating with someone, set out a blue cloth or paper with a spiral drawn on it. Hold a large piece of blue tiger's-eye in your hands, thinking of clearing away all the communication difficulties. Then, coax your playful cat to come over and visit. Roll the stone on the cloth, bat it back and forth with the cat, playing until the cat gets tired and walks away. Leave the stone on your altar most of the time, but keep it with you when you interact with the person. Once the situation is resolved, cleanse the stone and put it away.

Cerridwen Iris Shea

Spell for Safety

When feeling unsafe, say the guardian angel prayer:

Angel of Life,
My guardian dear.
To whom sweet love
Commits me here.
Ever this day
Be at my side
To light and guard
To rule and guide.

Therese Francis

18 July

Holly Driving Charm

To make a charm that will protect you as you drive, place the following items in a small box: three holly leaves, one clove of garlic, one sprig of cedar, one piece of clear quartz, and one piece of dragon's blood resin. Hold the box shut, and imagine you are driving your car. Envision yourself working in a clear, keen, and observant state. You make decisions as necessary when you are behind the wheel; you react with split-second timing, and you generally find joy in your role as a safe driver. Put the box in the glove compartment of your car and follow through by always driving in a safe and responsible manner.

Yasmine Galenorn

Spell to Boost Personal Productivity

To improve your own work productivity, during the waxing Moon place one hematite in a small basket or tray and enchant it by saying: "Ground and heal, magnetic one; bring me clarity on this day." Add the quartz crystal to the container and say: "Bring boundless energy to me; may it last through this day." Add the calcite and say: "Stone of joy and yellow light, help me sort through my work today." Place the container of stones on your desk and say: "Help me work through the day; bring me inspiration. And when the day is done, may the labor be finished."

Dorothy Morrison

20 July

Love and Admiration Oil

To make an oil that will help attract the attention of others, mix together twenty drops of synthetic musk, two drops of jasmine, and one drop of ylang ylang in a small bottle and leave where the full moonlight can strike it for three nights. Be sure to bring it inside before the Sun can find it. Meanwhile, leave a rose petal, a small piece of crystal quartz, and ⅛ teaspoon of powdered cinnamon in a place where the Sun can see them, making sure to move them before moonlight can strike them. On the fourth day, mix together the two sets of ingredients and leave in a dark place. Wear when you wish to draw love and admiration to yourself. It will also enable your employers to see what they love about your work for them.

deTraci Regula

Holey Stones Spell

Stones with a naturally occurring hole in them are considered good luck by many people. If you are so lucky as to find one, wear it around your neck by a cord through the hole. Silk or cotton cord is best; do not use a metal chain. Don't wrap wire around them, or otherwise tamper with them. Looking through the hole is said to give one the power of second sight and the ability to see the invisible world of the fey.

Magenta Griffith

22 July

Strong-as-an-Oak Spell

To increase your overall strength, at the New Moon in spring cut off a young oak twig, being sure to ask permission of the dryad beforehand. If refused, oak bark is available from many herbalists and is a respectable substitute. Strip the twig of its shiny bark, and place this or the store-bought dried bark in a saucepan of water. Boil until thoroughly infused. As you work, consider oaken qualities: fertility, sturdiness, durability, deep-rootedness. Know that in this brew, these properties are concentrated. If you are in full health and not pregnant, for optimum effect, take the potion as tea. If frail or if preferred, add to your bath. In both cases the important factor is to feel the properties of oak entering and fortifying your system. Entreat the spirit of the sacred tree to protect you. Using a ribbon and the leftover leaves, create a bouquet of thanks to this most ancient of benefactors.

Kala Trobe

Find a New Friend Spell

This spell works well for children who feel lonely. To find a new friend, sit in a safe place and get quiet. Then say out loud: "If I were my friend, where would I be?" Be quiet and wait for the answer.

Therese Francis

24 July

Protection Spell

Charge a small stone of Saturn correspondence to carry with you as a charm of protection— black tourmaline, Apache tears, or snowflake obsidian. Or find any dark colored stone in the earth that feels solid, stable, and strong to you. Find a quiet outdoor place and sprinkle a circle of salt on the ground, large enough for you to sit inside, and hold your chosen stone. Close your eyes; ground and center, drawing Earth energy within you. Visualize rings of energy swirling around the Saturn stone you hold, building and increasing to surround and emanate from you. Within the rings you are strong, solid, secure, and shielded from harm. In the future, whenever you feel the need for extra protection, hold your stone to assist you.

Maria Kay Simms

Bless Your Computer

Every day when you turn on your computer, take the time to be aware of all the technology that makes your modern-day life possible—telephones, refrigerators, electric lights, indoor plumbing, and central heating. Say a blessing to the inventors, creators, and builders that make your life possible. Thank your computer as the representative of all the technology in your life. You'll find that you have fewer problems when you regularly make this blessing.

Therese Francis

26 July

Silver Dollar Spell

To promote happiness and prosperity, take four silver dollars, bearing the current year if possible, and place them face up on the ground at the four corners of your home. Along with the coins, place some rue and vervain, a sprig of wheat, a few raw corn kernels, and a few pink or red rose petals. As you bury these things, say: "Bright coins, bless this house. Replace our worries with happiness and prosperity!" Do this during the waxing Moon for best results.

Lori Bruno

July 27

Banishing a Love Rival

This spell from New Orleans encourages a love rival to turn his or her attention elsewhere and is best done on Friday or Saturday night during a waning or New Moon. Beginning after sundown, gather some raw meat a little past its prime, something "broken," some angelica, a garlic clove, and a leek. Tie these items together in a cheesecloth bound by black thread. On the outside paint the letter "X" three times in dragon's blood ink. Douse the entire charm, known as a gris-gris in New Orleans, in lime juice. Before dawn, take the charm to your rival's home and toss it onto the lawn saying: "By this spell, you must find a love that steals your heart and mind. Turn your heart from my love, and make a new start."

Edain McCoy

28 July

Folklore Spell

To honor the folk traditions of your people today, hold a folklore party with friends or family
members who share your traditions. Serve traditional foods, and dress in appropriate clothes if
you have them. Sing favorite songs about folk he-
roes or practices. Take turns reciting or reading
aloud folktales that you love. Tell your life story as
a folktale, with yourself as the protagonist. Dis-
cuss or study the customs, superstitions, and folk
magic of your people. At the beginning and end
of the celebration, and between the various activities, chant this rhyme to help focus energy on
the transmission of folklore: "Tell me a story, or
sing me a song. Teach me the old ways we've kept
so long." This spell makes it easier and more fun
to learn folklore. It may be performed at any time
of the year, indoors or outdoors.

Elizabeth Barrette

Getting Rid of Cramps Spell

To get rid of premenstrual cramps, add three to five drops of ylang ylang essential oil to a cup of hot water. As you do so, imagine standing under a waterfall, smelling the fragrant ylang ylang herb. Sip the tea and continue to imagine yourself under the warm waterfall. As the water streams over your body, let it wash away the cramps.

Therese Francis

30 July

Banishment Stirring Spell

If you need to banish something from your life,
prepare a pot of soup. Draw a banishing pentagram in the soup, then stir nine times counter-
clockwise, saying: "Blessed Lord, gracious Lady,
hear my plea. Remove (insert what needs re-
moval) from me. For the good of all, with harm to
none; once this is eaten, the spell is done!" Eat the
soup. If it is an interpersonal conflict and you have
the other person's permission, share the soup.

Cerridwen Iris Shea

Unwanted Visitor Spell

My mother taught me that to get rid of unwanted visitors, you should place a broom by the front door. If you can, make a small sweeping motion as you place the broom, and if you can do this without being noticed, so much the better. This will speed such people on their way and give you some peace of mind.

Magenta Griffith

1 August

Lammas Ritual

An old Pagan custom associated with Lammas is the making of a corn doll from the last sheaf of corn from a harvest. For good luck throughout the coming twelve months, the corn doll is traditionally hung up in the kitchen or in the chimney, and kept there until the following Lammas, when it is ritually burned. It is said that if the previous year's corn doll is not removed before Christmas, the next harvest will be a poor one. To make a traditional Witch's corn doll for good luck, twist or tie together a few husks of corn into a small female figure. If desired, you may dress the corn doll and decorate it with dried flowers. Anoint it with a few drops of frankincense or clove oil, and then pass it twelve times through the smoke of burning sage to consecrate it as you chant your intent over it.

Gerina Dunwich

August 2

Group Project Ritual

Oh, goody—you've been assigned to work on a group project! Now you need to find a way to get everyone to work together—easier said than done! Still, there are several magical steps you can take to aid the process. First, on the evening before the project begins, bake "harmony" cookies for your project-mates—sugar cookies, cut in heart shapes and sprinkled with vanilla sugar, will work well for this. Then, before leaving for work in the morning, look in the mirror and see a patient, cooperative, and efficient team player. Wear rose, carnation, or musk cologne, and a red carnation in your buttonhole, and bring a bouquet of roses, carnations, or geraniums to the board-room table. Suggest lunch at an Italian or Thai restaurant where they use lots of basil. Now, you should be ready to reap the rewards of increased cooperation and team effort in the workplace.

Denise Dumars

3 August

The Love-Bath Spell

Start this spell on a Friday evening at seven o'clock by adorning your bathroom with one red rose in a water-filled vase and seven pale green candles. Run the bath water, and honor Venus by adding to it one cup of sweet amber honey, one cup of pink wine, a splash of rose-scented perfume, and several drops of myrtle and clover essential oils. Next, get undressed, light the candles, turn off the light, and enter the tub. Allow the warm delicious water to soothe your muscles and your spirit. Imagine that your lover finds you beautiful, impossible to resist, and is ready to submit to your charms. When the visualization is complete, drain the water from the tub and stand under a cool shower. This will further magnetize your body and draw your lover to you.

Marguerite Elsbeth

Freedom Spell

For a freedom spell, light a brightly colored candle and meditate on the freedoms you have in your life. In which areas of your life do you have complete autonomy? Where are you constrained by other people, or by situations beyond your control? Can you get unencumbered and become freer? Sometimes we end up being owned by possessions or people and don't even realize it. Thank the cosmos for your freedoms and evaluate where you have chosen to anchor yourself. Give yourself permission to do what you want for a day.

Estelle Daniels

5 August

Leo Energy Spell

Use the following sunshine spell to help with gathering motivation, dealing with children, giving the gift of unconditional love, or shining at your workplace. To begin, find an old CD that you no longer wish to play. Place gold foil or old gold Christmas wrapping paper over the CD and fold around the edges. Over the CD, sprinkle the following mixture: dried crushed sunflower or marigold petals, yellow powder, gold glitter, and dried orange peel. With your finger or a pencil, write the symbols of the Sun (☉) and Leo (♌) in the mixture. Allow the Sun to shine on your project for at least thirty minutes; then place a gold candle on the CD and allow candle to burn completely. Reaffirm your petition throughout the day as you gaze at the candle for a few moments. Put the CD wherever you wish to shine—your office, work room, home, or vehicle.

Silver RavenWolf

August 6

Table Blessing

Before starting to eat, look at the food on your plate deliberately. Then bless the food by saying: "For light and life and all good things, I thank you."

Therese Francis

7 August

Herbal Witches Cleansing Bottle

To make an herbal cleansing bottle, pour a layer of clean sand into a large clear bottle. Add layers of dried herbs, one at a time: first rosemary; then lemon peel, sage, cedar, black peppercorns, lavender, dill, bay leaf, and rowan. When the bottle is full, focus cleansing protective energy into the herbs and sand, and see a golden light radiating from the bottle. Visualize the herbs driving away negative influences. Cork and seal the bottle with white wax. Using a permanent marker, draw the Algiz rune on one side of the bottle, and on the other side draw a pentagram. Set the bottle near your front or back door, and every six months, uncap, pour herbs out into the woods or your compost heap, and thoroughly wash and dry the bottle before filling it with a new round of herbs.

Yasmine Galenorn

August 8

A Spell to Enhance Listening

We can all learn to listen better. When we make that effort, the other party is motivated to try harder too. If you and someone else are not understanding each other, at least make sure the fault does not lie with your inability to listen. Before meeting someone, cleanse your ears carefully and chant: "Release the need, let go desire; personal wants shall all be banned, save the need to understand." Resolve that your only task is truly to understand what the other party wants and feels. During the conversation listen carefully. Repeat back to the person what you think you heard, paraphrased in your own words, and ask questions when you need to. When the other party is finished, and you both agree that your understanding is correct, wait for a moment and think deeply about the other's viewpoint before you respond.

Amber K

9 August

Visualization for Job Interview Success

You're ready for the job interview. You've got your power suit on, your resume in your briefcase, and your hair is just so. Wait a minute; haven't you forgotten something? Add a sachet of comfrey and sage—both sacred to Jupiter—to your briefcase. Then before you leave for that interview, try this visualization: Sit in front of a mirror, preferably full-length, in your business clothes. Pretend you are the employer, looking at the prospective employee sitting across from you. Visualize this person doing the job that needs filling; see him or her doing it well, being an asset to the organization and making the boss proud. Now, say aloud: "This is a competent person. This is a professional person. This is a perfect candidate for this job." Then smile at yourself in the mirror, get up, and go get that new job!

Denise Dumars

Spell to Add Zest to a Long-Term Relationship

To add zest to a long-term relationship, working alone light five spice-scented candles, surrounding yourself in a circle of fragrant light. Pour grape seed oil into a small bowl, saying: "Our foundation is a sure vessel, but it can carry more spice." Add seven drops of sandalwood oil, saying: "Sensual scent of ancient sanders, bless our union." Add three drops of orange oil, saying: "Newlywed playfulness, bless this union;" add three drops of geranium oil, saying: "Banal troubles flee, let our love be free." Pass the bowl over each candle flame, mentally enlivening the love-balm with vibrant fire-qualities as you go. When you are both ready for magic, light all of the candles, lay your lover on the bed and massage with the oil, picturing as you do so what exactly you wish from the relationship. Now work your will on your pliant partner.

Kala Trobe

11 August

The Wizard of Oz

Have you ever read *The Wizard of Oz* by L. Frank Baum? If you've just seen the movie, take the time to read the book. If you've read it, all of the dozen or so other Oz books Baum wrote are worth reading. Most of them are still in print nearly a century after they were written. Libraries and secondhand bookstores are good sources for Oz books, too. All magic needs imagination, and books like these develop yours. Give the child in you a treat!

Magenta Griffith

August 12

Purring Cat Spell

For a health-giving spell, lie down where you will be comfortable and undisturbed for a half hour or so. Place your cat on your chest, covering your heart chakra. State your positive intent to be healthy succinctly and begin to stroke the cat. The cat should relax and begin to purr. Completely relax with the cat and let the purring cleanse out your heart chakra. After about thirty minutes, sit up and send the positive intent out into the universe.

Cerridwen Iris Shea

13 August

House Blessing

Prepare your home and yourself for the onset of spring by first cleaning house the conventional way. As you do, meditate on the mental detritus you need to clean out as well. Then, when you're ready, take up your ritual broom, start at the front door and sweep all around the house, visualizing all unwanted things being swept away by your magical broom. When you return to the front door, open it wide and sweep this stuff away. Now light a white candle and carry it around your home. Visualize a light of peace and newness spreading around you and your home. Make a circle of light before each window and door, asking the blessings of the Goddess and the God on your home and all who dwell within it.

Maria Kay Simms

Spells to Keep Away Moths

If you don't want to use mothballs to preserve your winter woolens, here are some herbal charms that have been used for ages to keep moths away. The best remedy against moths, and indeed against many kinds of insects, is pennyroyal. Sachets made with this herb will keep away moths, and the essential oil is a frequent ingredient in herbal bug-repellent. Lavender also keeps away moths and other bugs, and imparts a wonderful fragrance to clothing and bedding. Cedar is excellent for keeping clothes intact; that's why people use cedar chests. If you can't afford a cedar chest, you can often find blocks of cedar that will serve the same purpose.

Magenta Griffith

15 August

Spell for Bringing a Computer into Your Life

This spell for blessing a new computer is intended only for when Mercury is direct. To affect the spell, cut out pictures of the computer, software programs, and peripherals you want from a computer catalog. Tape or glue them onto a piece of cardboard, and when finished place the cardboard where you will have the computer after it arrives. Light a silver candle and pray to the spirit of computers and the planets Mercury and Uranus to allow this computer to take up permanent residence in your life.

Therese Francis

August 16

Rue & Vervain Prosperity Bag

To make a powerful prosperity pouch, obtain a
rue plant and a vervain plant from a local nursery.
Make a small pouch of bright red velvet, cotton,
or silk, and in this red bag put coarse salt. Stitch
the pouch closed. Then, form a larger red bag
with a drawstring of red cord. Into this bag,
loosely place the little pouch containing the salt,
some rue leaves, and some vervain. This bag will
bring you both prosperity and protection.

Lori Bruno

17 August

Candles for a Passionate Love Spell

To draw a passionate love your way, during a waxing Moon gather two taper candles, one pink and one red, and some red thread and jasmine oil. Anoint the candles with jasmine oil using your fingertips; then light them while visualizing the flames of passion growing between yourself and new, but yet unknown, love. Link the candles together by making a figure eight between them with the thread while saying over and over: "Flames of passion and seeds of romance grow; I open my heart to love. Now the one who seeks me shall come." For best results, enact the spell on three consecutive nights.

Edain McCoy

August 18

Buried Treasure Spell

To bring buried treasure into your life, make a list of six local places which have good associations for you. They can be places you've visited, or places that have always sounded interesting. Map them out on a local map, and then choose your route. From each place, bring away something: A memory of a pleasant walk, a fallen leaf, a silly souvenir or memento. Remember, however, that the pirate's life holds no promises, and some of the places you choose may be disappointing or dangerous. But of the six you list, at least one spot is guaranteed to hold an unexpected treasure for you!

deTraci Regula

19 August

August Harvest Meditation

In France, the first harvest was celebrated in honor of the god Lugus. The town named for him was Lugudunum, which eventually became Lyons. Under Roman influence, harvest celebrations were held in honor of the emperor Augustus from whom we get the name of the month. In our modern world it's easy to forget how important a successful harvest was to our ancestors. A good harvest meant survival during the dark cold months. A poor harvest was the beginning of difficult times, famine, or death. This is a good time to give thought to where our food originates and reverence for the cycles that produce it. Better still, tending a garden keeps us in touch with the Goddess and her bounty. Even tomatoes and herbs grown in pots on a windowsill taste all the sweeter for having been nurtured by our own energy.

Sedwin

Creating-a-Familiar Spell

This rite is designed specifically for cats, but may be employed with any animal you wish to make your familiar spirit. Each night during the cycle of the waxing Moon, sit closely with the animal. Arrange it so that you are both facing toward the horizon where the Moon shall rise. Stroke the creature firmly, but with love, until he or she begins to purr or to relax. Align your own breathing with the purr, or in the case of a creature other than a feline friend, align your breathing with that of the animal. Continue to do this each night at moonrise. When the Moon is at full, your will shall be as one with that of your familiar. You shall see through its eyes, and it will see through yours. Your thoughts shall be as one, and you will share a single heart.

Gwyndion O'Hara

21 August

Create a Turquoise Amulet

The ancients regarded turquoise as a powerful magical aid to ward off misfortune, illness, and the evil eye. You can use turquoise to make your own amulet for protection. To begin, during the waxing Moon take a piece of blue turquoise or an item of blue turquoise jewelry and hold it in your hand for a moment. In your mind's eye, picture a blue light surrounding you. Hold the stone to your heart, and breathe on it to charge it with your power, saying: "Stone of blue, surround me with protective energy. I am protected by your soothing blue light." Carry your turquoise with you or wear it as often as you can. Handle it frequently to keep the spell active.

Jim Weaver

August 22

Car Blessing

Before leaving on a lengthy journey, bless your car. Walk around it clockwise and examine the body, the windows, the wheels, and so on. Imagine yourself storing up more and more energy within yourself with each breath that you take, then breathe out all of the energy, fixing it in each of the car's parts. Say aloud, "May the protection of the Lord and the Lady be in and about this vehicle, that it may deliver us safe to our destination. So mote it be!" Then get in and drive off.

Ed Fitch

23 August

Cats and Money

Cats can be harbingers of coming prosperity and good fortune. A cat of three colors is extremely lucky and will keep a house from harm, while a smutty-nosed cat will bring wealth to its companions. Stroking a cat's tail nine times grants good luck at cards. And just sharing your home with cats will bring you many blessings.

Scott Cunningham

August 24

Walking Through the Threshold

The threshold of a building has always held its own magical energy, and it can be utilized to heighten the interest of a potential romantic partner. To draw your new love interest to your home, during a waxing Moon take some talc or corn starch and mix with finely ground love herbs such as vanilla, clove, lavender, jasmine, yarrow, thyme, myrtle, and rue. Visualize the goal as you mix. Sprinkle the area around your threshold to draw your potential lover while chanting: "Through my doorway comes my love, drawn in rapture, drawn to stay; feet enchanted by my spell are ever drawn to this place." As he or she walks over the powder, visualize it sticking to his feet so that he or she will continue to be drawn to your home.

Edain McCoy

25 August

Spell for a Summer Drought

Use this spell to ease a summer drought. You can cast it when no rain is in sight, when rain has been predicted but has not appeared, or when it is raining but someone else is trying to send the much-needed rain away. Go outside and do any of the things that folklore associates with bringing rain, such as washing your car or hanging a load of laundry on the clothesline. While you work, chant this variant of a classic rhyme: "Rain, rain, come and stay; fall all night and fall all day!" Put as much passion as you can into the chant. When enough rain has fallen, use the original version to clear the skies: "Rain, rain, go away; come again another day!" When working weather magic, it is essential to invite the rain back later; otherwise it may take offense and stay away, causing another drought.

Elizabeth Barrette

August 26

The Siren's Song Bath Spell

To create a layer of magnetism and charm in your aura as you bathe, on your vanity counter lay out an altar with a crystal dish holding various seashells and pretty ocean rocks—seven blue, green, and lavender votive candles in clear containers—and any other ocean-oriented treasures you might have. Fill the tub with water and light-scented bath salts and bubble bath, and light the candles. Stand in front of your mirror, and look at yourself in the candlelight. Visualize a halo of sea foam and pearls around you. Take a deep breath and imagine you are breathing in the essence of Aphrodite, the foam-born. Then settle into the tub and take a long slow bath, luxuriating in the feel of the bubbles and bath oils. Sing, if you like, or play soft sensuous music to contribute to the mood.

Yasmine Galenorn

27 August

Call a Household Pet

If you are interested in a certain kind of animal, say a poodle or angora cat, gather everyone in your household together for this ten-minute ritual. First, light a votive candle. Say in a loud voice, "We want a poodle (or other type of animal) to be here with us." Have everyone mention something they intend to offer the pet—love, time, walks in the park, play, snuggling, food. Together take a few quiet moments to visualize life with the imagined pet. Then blow out the candle, and exclaim, "Welcome to our home!" Follow your hunches about where and when to find your new household member.

Therese Francis

Gremlin Banishment Spell
(for Washer and Dryer)

Technological advances have gotten ahead of magic in many ways; there are few specific spells to protect modern machines. This is bad because gremlins just love machines. They get inside and cause all manner of mayhem. Gremlins are especially fond of appliances like washers and dryers, where they chew holes in your clothes, add inexplicable spots, and pilfer socks, leaving you with unmatched pairs. To banish gremlins from your washer and dryer, first tie a long sock into three knots. Then add nine pinches of salt to the wash water. Wash and dry the load as usual. When you take the clothes out of the dryer, check the sock—if all the knots are untied, then all the gremlins are gone; and if any of the knots remain, there are still some gremlins left. Repeat the charm as needed to banish any remaining gremlins.

Elizabeth Barrette

29 August

Luggage Arrival Spell

To ensure that luggage arrives with you when traveling, knot a teaspoon of lavender into a handkerchief for each piece of luggage while chanting something like: "Lavender, attune and fix this bag, and protect it from tricks. Make sure it goes where I am going, so it meets me at my destination." Place one sachet in each bag.

Dorothy Morrison

Found Penny Spell

The following spell, which takes years to complete, affirms the flow of energy into your life by hailing every found penny as a symbol of continued abundance. Each time you find a penny, pick it up and say: "Thanks for good fortune!" When you have 999 pennies, a special magic will be released to bolster your abundance. Add a penny to make 1,000; then take them to the bank to be converted into a crisp $10 bill. (999 represents the multiplication of power, but 1,000 and 10 are also lucky as they correspond to 1, which is the Sun's number.) Ten minutes after the next New Moon, write the following words on the $10 bill: "I take in the infinite abundance of this universe." You can then frame it or fold it and sew it between two squares of green felt to use as a charm.

Janina Renée

31 August

To-Feel-Loved Spell

We all are in need of love sometimes. To tap into the flowing current of love in the universe, place a few rose quartz crystals in cold water in your bath for as long as possible. The longer they soak, the stronger the effect. Fill a pink bottle with the water and place in direct sunlight. Again, leave it as long as possible. When it is ready, light a few red, pink, or white candles, and run the bath, sprinkling in a pinch of salt as you visualize the water glowing white. Now vivify the water with seven drops of rose oil. Finally add the bottled water, and watch as it spreads bright pink light through the bath. As you get in, feel the color and warmth spreading through every inch of your body. Relax and enjoy it.

Kala Trobe

September 1

A Tarot Divination

You will only need the major arcana portion of your deck for this reading. As you shuffle and cut the major arcana cards ask the question you have in mind. Then, pick up the cards while keeping them facedown. Working in a clockwise direction, lay each card facedown forming a large circle with enough space in the center to hold three cards. Then, in a clockwise motion circle your power hand over the cards and say three times: "Round and round the tarot wheel, let the truth be revealed!" At the end of each statement, stop your hand above a card at random and place that card facedown in the center of the circle. Select two more cards, placing them from right to left, then turn each card faceup from right to left. The far right card is your past, the middle card, your present situation, and the left card will reveal your possible future outcome.

Jim Weaver

2 September

Journey Spell

For a spell to take you on a spiritual journey, find a peaceful spot at home to meditate on traveling to a new place. The place may be real or in your head. Afterward, light a pastel-colored candle and meditate about your journey. Ask yourself how it healed or renewed you. Think about how such mini-journeys can refresh and renew your outlook on life and bring peace to your hectic day. Take a bubble bath by candlelight and daydream about happy things.

Estelle Daniels

September 3

Home Blessing

To bless your home, first, if you have not done so already, cleanse it thoroughly. Then, take a censer containing your favorite scent, a bell, and a small bowl of salted water. Waft the incense, ring the bell, and flick the water into every room and nook of the house, remembering the plug-holes, the toilet, and the chimney. Visualize as you do that all hostile spirits are fleeing and negative energy of the past is being nullified. You may wish to allow friendly spirits to stay since they will not interfere with your life. Now, stand at the center of every room and burn a little frankincense combined with a few drops of rose oil, and say: "This room is a sanctuary of love and health. Here, beneficent forces prosper. Here is our homestead, and may Hestia, Venus, and Jupiter bless it."

Kala Trobe

4 September

Spell to Cleanse Crystals

To cleanse your citrine, quartz, rose quartz, or amethyst crystals, fill the bathtub or a large basin with room-temperature water. The temperature is very important, as too cold or hot water can cause the crystals to crack. Next, add one cup of salt to the bathtub, or about ¼ cup salt if you are using a basin. Gently place your crystals in the water and let soak for at least an hour. Use a toothbrush to scrub any dirt or grime from the face of the crystals. After you drain the water, rinse the crystals in lukewarm water and then, if possible, set them in sunlight to dry.

Yasmine Galenorn

September 5

The Scarlet Letter Spell

When you mail a job resume or other important document, you want your letter to be noticed. Apart from using a colored envelope or big commemorative stamp, what can you do? Well, you can get some powdered ginseng (it comes as an herbal supplement at health food stores). Then, cast a circle and light a red candle. If possible, play some trumpet music, or anything lively with lots of brass and drums. Dust the ginseng lightly over your envelope and visualize the envelope glowing a brilliant red. Pass the envelope over the candle several times (not close enough to scorch it or get smoke on it!), and chant: "Crimson and gules, scarlet and red, incarnadined letter, seen clear and read." Mail your letter as soon as possible. The energy charge will draw attention to your letter.

Edain McCoy

6 September

Virgo Energy Spell

The ultimate fixer, Virgo uses the ability to discern and analyze to solve any problem. To tap into Virgo energy, find an unused check register. On the first page, list your ancestors. On the next page, write the current date in the "date" column. State your dilemma in the "description of transaction" column. Under the "balance" column write your hoped-for solution. On the front of the transaction register, draw the symbol for Mercury (☿) and the symbol for Virgo (♍). Wrap a rubber band around the register and snap it three times, repeating your desires. Each day, write down the mundane steps you have taken to solve the problem. Remember to wrap the rubber band around the register when you are finished, and snap the band three times. When your problem is solved you should bury the register in your back yard.

Silver RavenWolf

September 7

A Lotion Love–Potion

Commercially prepared body lotions can be easily transformed into magical potions to attract love your way. During a waxing Moon, place one level cup of any kind of lotion into a clean eight-ounce jar, and add a teaspoon of vanilla extract, three drops jasmine oil, two teaspoons grated lemon peel, 1/8 teaspoon ground cinnamon, and one or two drops nutmeg or anise oil. Blend the lotion with your fingers while visualizing your magical goal. Rub your clean body with the lotion before you go out to find a new romance. As you rub in the lotion say: "I prepare myself to find romance. I seek my partner in eternal dance. Love and romance, where I may be, I seek to find and draw to me."

Edain McCoy

8 September

Spell Against Graffiti

If there is some ugly graffiti that offends your senses, then imagine strongly in your mind that the creator of these scrawls is standing before them. Drawing in thirteen or more breaths of energy and directing it with your right hand, weave a silver cocoon of energy about both the graffiti and its creator, imaging clearly that he is bound firmly in with his creation. Let him then stew in his own juice until he changes to become a better person. It may be useful to then attach the cocoon to a tree or patch of grass or a potted plant, so that the plant may gain strength from whatever is within.

Ed Fitch

September 9

Ending Short-Term Depression Spell

To alleviate the effects of short-term depression, light a yellow candle and meditate on how you feel right now. Give this feeling a name—such as "Gus." The sillier the name, the better. Then, light a green candle. Meditate on how you feel now that you've named the previous feeling. Give this new feeling a name. Again, silly is good. After lighting a blue candle, meditate on how you feel now that you've named the previous feeling. Repeat the routine. Finally, light a red candle. Know that you have control over what you do with your emotions, just as you have control over choosing names for your emotions. Now you can allow yourself to be aware of what started the depression. For most people, something happened that initially caused anger and then caused fear.

Therese Francis

10 September

Running with the Pack

If you are at a farm or ranch where there is a pack of friendly dogs, cement your friendship with them by greeting them daily and perhaps feeding them. At a Full Moon, dress yourself in rugged clothing with some fur (false or real), and go out into the moonlight to find your friends. Go for a walk with them, or find a place where you and your pack of friends feel comfortable. If they begin to howl at the Moon, then you should do so also. Or you might want to start the pack howl yourself, since canines usually love the music and the magic of such an experience.

Ed Fitch

Four Thieves Banishing

While banishings are of questionable karmic wisdom, there are times when one is faced with choosing the lesser of evils. In this event, let your conscience be your guide. This banishing spell was created by Marie Laveau and draws on the traditions of New Orleans voodoo. To start, write the name of the undesirable individual on a piece of parchment. Place this into a bottle and cover it with Four Thieves Vinegar, which is made by placing a handful of vetivert, some black pepper, High John root, and Adam and Eve root into a base of red wine vinegar. Seal the bottle, and throw it into a body of moving water, such as a river or a stream. Queen Laveau asserts that as the bottle is carried off by the moving water, so shall the undesirable be removed from the location.

Gwydion O'Hara

12 September

Spell for Saying No

If you are inclined to say "yes" too often, and often regret it, you may make a "No Way" talisman. This would be a tiny pouch worn about your neck, stuffed with little papers on which you've written words and phrases such as "No," "Never," "Nyet," "Nein," "I think not," "Not in a billion years," and so on. Charge the talisman by drumming at the dark of the Moon. Next, lightly touch your lower lip and say "no" very firmly. Do it again and say "I think not," and repeat such phrases one hundred times. The next time anyone asks you for anything, touch your lower lip in exactly the same way, and touch your talisman (through your shirt) with the other hand. You will have the power to refuse—if you choose to.

Amber K

September 13

Ginger Tea

Ginger is a warm, fragrant spice. It is also a powerful money attractant, as is the cinnamon in this recipe.

Tea

 5 cups water
 ⅓ cup fresh ginger root, peeled and thinly
  sliced
 ¾ cup sugar
 ½ teaspoon cinnamon, ground

Add the ginger to the water in a large saucepan. Boil for twenty minutes. Strain, and add sugar and cinnamon. Stir and serve.

Scott Cunningham

14 September

Pink Love Spell

Pink lends strength to an uncertain relationship, and enhances romantic love. Prepare an altar space, and place two pink candles, a flat plate covered with earth, and one pink rose in a water-filled vase upon it. Plant the candles in the dirt on the plate so that their stems are touching from the base to the tips. Place the rose in front of the plate, then light the candles and gaze at the flames and the rose. Surround your relationship with feelings of joy, happiness, forgiveness, and love. Mentally embrace and release your lover, allowing her the freedom to choose to stay in the relationship or not. Allow the candles to melt down until the flames extinguish. If your lover is willing, you will both be back in the pink within three days time.

Marguerite Elsbeth

September 15

Autumn Meditation

For this meditation, which takes advantage of autumn's inward-turning energy to help you contemplate life and afterlife, you need an image of the goddess White Tara, plus a suitable incense like nag champa or patchouli. Begin with this invocation: "Tara, star goddess, eternally burning one—fuel our hunger for knowledge, prepare us for release from the merely physical, and ferry us across from the world of delusion to the world of truth. White Tara, bright Tara, we beseech you: Open your three eyes to the deeds of our lives and teach us to see beyond death to freedom." Spend at least ten minutes meditating on the meaning of life and the infinite possibilities of the afterlife. You may find it helpful to gaze at the goddess image or the smoke, or you may prefer to close your eyes. Afterward, thank White Tara for her help and let the incense burn out.

Elizabeth Barrette

16 September

Psychic Dreaming Spell

To encourage psychic dreaming, sew a small pillow and stuff with mugwort, lavender buds, rose petals, and a few drops of rose oil. Place under your regular pillow, and brew a tea of chamomile with a pinch of powdered cinnamon and thyme, flavored with honey if you choose. Put paper and pen beside your bed, sip the tea, and repeat three times: "Herbs of magic, herbs of peace, bring dreams of mystic sight. When I wake, bring memory, wisdom, truth, and light." On awakening in the morning, pause a few moments to recall your dream. Write down what you remember. Rereading later often brings insights not immediately clear to you on wakening. You are the best interpreter of your own dreams.

Maria Kay Simms

Environmental Protection Amulet

Gather together fallen feathers, dried twigs, leaves, and flowers from as many species as possible in your area. Play with what you have gathered, so you become intimately familiar with each piece—the patterns of the plants, the softness of the feathers, the smell of the flowers and twigs. With a piece of grass, or a thick thread or string, bind the materials together, enchanting them as you do so by saying: "All things are magic; to ignore them is tragic. All things, high and low, are to be protected. With this little charm, I protect all from harm." Hang the charm up, or place it in a dry bud vase where you can see it every day. Each time you view it, send out your love and protective power over all the species and things it represents.

de Traci Regula

18 September

Renewing the Spirit Spell

In Hebrew the word for the process of purifying the self is *kiddishin*, meaning "sanctification." To begin your spiritual new year, whenever it might fall, start with a purification bath, known as mik-vah in Hebrew. Light some candles and burn an incense to assist with spiritual awareness such as sandalwood, myrrh, or frankincense. Mix up a small amount of nonirritating herbs and oils that share affinities with spirituality and purification such as olive oil, lemon juice, peppermint leaves, vervain, chamomile, hyssop, or rosemary. As you soak, visualize the impurities of spirit being pulled from you so that they can be washed down the drain. Follow the bath with a private rededication ritual to your spiritual path.

Edain McCoy

September 19

Travel-by-Water Talisman

If traveling by water, you may find protection by gathering the following items:

- A small silver or blue cloth bag
- A bit of paper with the signs of Venus and Neptune drawn on it
- A twig of rowan wood
- A tiny cork
- A bit of driftwood
- A small shell or piece of abalone
- A tiny wood, clay, or plastic dolphin

At the Full Moon, assemble the items on your altar, cast a circle round them, and charge the items by chanting: "Venus, Neptune, blessed be. Protect your child upon the sea; like a dolphin roam, and come safely home. Protect your child upon the sea. Venus, Neptune, blessed be!" Place the items in the bag and carry it with you on your voyage.

Amber K

20 September

Silver Coin Bath

Baths are very popular in magic. This may be because they act as a reunion with the element of water—after all, our bodies are mostly water. To promote prosperity in particular, place some silver coins in your bath to ensure money in the future. Many folks observe this practice at their baby's first bath. Fill the tub one-third full. Stand before the water, looking down. Charge the water by visualizing an abundance of money. Then slip into the water and know that the energy is merging with yours.

Scott Cunningham

September 21

Meditation to Create a Telepathic Link with Your Partner

You can work alone or together with your partner to create a telepathic link. Obviously, working with your partner will enhance your mutual bond, though the exercise is effective either way. To begin, take several deep breaths. When you are relaxed and focused, concentrate on your base chakra, and picture it opening directly onto your partner's chakra until two spinning red lights merge. Do the same with the orange intestinal chakra, the yellow solar plexus zone, the green heart chakra, blue throat area, violet third-eye, and finally the brilliant white of the crown chakra. See how the bands of light flow and interact, and be aware of your bodies as vessels for these centers of high-level communication. Repeat as desired. You will soon find that synchronicity is flowing between you and your partner.

Kala Trobe

22 September

Autumn Leaf Spell

In the fall, write a secret wish upon a fallen leaf. Choose a leaf with red colors for a wish pertaining to matters of love, sex, passion, or health; a gold-colored one for wishes involving money; a brown one for protection; a purple one for healing; an orange one for energy; a yellow one for confidence, attraction, or persuasion; a green one for fertility, success, or good luck. Fold the leaf in half (or roll it up) and seal it with a kiss. Using the flame of a white candle, set the leaf on fire. As it burns, visualize your wish coming true for you.

Gerina Dunwich

September 23

Sun Child Blessing

Because the Sun promotes growth and health, a Sun image is an appropriate charm for blessing a child. It is easy to find jewelry, pillows, candle holders, and other objects with Sun images. The Sun card from a tarot deck can also be used as an amulet. This card pertains to the birth and well-being of children, as some older French cards show two children dancing beneath the Sun while some newer versions feature a carefree child riding a horse. Empower your object by holding it to the Sun when you have good light. Visualize it being filled with warmth and power while saying: "Child of light, with eyes so bright, grow strong in health and wholeness." At the same time, visualize the child in question surrounded by a radiant golden aura.

Janina Renée

24 September

New Pot Blessing

To bless a new pot and promote a healthy growth of plants therein, light your favorite incense. Draw a pentagram on the inside and outside bottom of the pot with a wooden spoon, saying: "Blessings of earth for abundance." Pass the pot through the incense, saying: "Blessings of air for fragrance." Turn on the burner of your stove and place the pot on the flame carefully, saying: "Blessings of fire for purity in preparation." Stir in a little water, saying: "Blessings of water for love." Prepare a favorite food and share it.

Cerridwen Iris Shea

September 25

A Folk Cure for the Evil Eye

To break the curse of the evil eye assemble a white candle, ¼ cup water, ½ teaspoon olive oil, one small bowl, and nine whole cloves. Mix the water and olive oil in the bowl, and light the candle, visualizing yourself surrounded by a circle of protection. Pick up one clove at a time and hold it by the stem end so the bud end is directly above the tip of the candle's flame. It should ignite instantly. Immediately drop the burning clove into the water-oil mixture to extinguish it. Repeat with remaining cloves. The smoke and scent released by the smoldering cloves will repel any evil directed at you. When done, pour the clove and water mixture onto the ground so the negativity will be purified by the earth.

Jim Weaver

26 September

*Hands of Isis Spell for
Safe Travel by Air*

To ensure a safe flight, center yourself as the plane taxis to the runway. As the engines power up for takeoff, imagine the Egyptian goddess Isis—huge in stature—looming behind the airplane. She is large enough to hold the plane in her cupped hand. Visualize her with raven-black hair and eyes, a gauzy white gown, and huge colorful wings. Say quietly to yourself: "Isis, with your rainbow wings, Isis, with your loving hands, protect us all in this flight; hold this aircraft till it lands." When the plane accelerates down the runway, Isis leans forward and places her hands beneath the plane as it lifts from the ground. Her wings spread and she soars forth into the sky, gently holding the aircraft aloft. All the way to your destination, know that she flies with you and keeps you safe. As the plane touches down, give her thanks.

Amber K

September 27

Circle of Atonement Spell

In Hebrew tradition, forgiveness is granted to one who fasts and prays over wrongs done over the past year. Forgiveness is only granted if the supplicant has sought and obtained forgiveness from people she has wronged. Make yourself aware of your wrongdoings by creating a written list of them. Take this and some bread to a lake or river. Bury or burn your list while visualizing the bread absorbing these wrongs. Focus on each wrongdoing as you break off small portions of the bread, casting them into the water to be carried away from you, saying: "As what goes out always comes back, I do both give and ask forgiveness. Purity of spirit shall live in me; I give what I get, so mote it be."

Edain McCoy

28 September

Love Medicine Pouch Spell

To make a pouch that beckons a perfect lover, begin by facing east. Moving clockwise, cast a magic circle and call upon the powers of the four directions—in order, east, south, west, north—as you turn. Now, place four white candles around the circle, one at each of the four directions, and position a red candle in front of you behind a chalice or crystal wine glass. Light all the candles. Have ready a piece of plain white paper, and write down all the qualities you want in a potential lover. Prepare and ignite an incense using the herbs cardamom and clove. Burn the paper containing your lover's qualities along with the incense, until all turns to ashes. Put the ashes in a red silk pouch, to be worn around your neck. Kiss the pouch frequently throughout the day, remembering what you want as you do so.

Marguerite Elsbeth

September 29

Cloud Divination

In the wilderness, on a day when there are fluffy clouds in the sky, you may enact this divination. To start, fix your mind on something you wish to know, and look down at the forest floor for about five minutes or so. Then look up at the sky and see what shapes the clouds suggest. Interpret what you see based on what you want to know.

Ed Fitch

30 September

Spell for Mental Inspiration

To increase your general feelings of inspiration, during a waxing Moon anoint a yellow candle with vanilla oil and roll it in a few teaspoons of thyme. Light the candle while chanting: "Muses hear my call, inspire and enchant me. When at last I am infused with new ideas, may I have a fresh perspective." Let the candle burn down completely.

Dorothy Morrison

Stirring Spell

Whenever you stir something on the stove or in a mixing bowl, use a wooden spoon. Draw a pentacle in the food and stir it nine times, saying: "The blessings of the mother, the strength of the father, imbue this food with love and grace to all who in good faith partake." After the final stir, add: "So mote it be."

Cerridwen Iris Shea

2 October

Sukkot begins

Spell for Getting Active

For a spell to get active, start by exercising, cleaning house, and taking on sweaty projects. Expend energy in some way or it may manifest in negative ways—angry words or minor mishaps. Feel your muscles moving, your body working. Breathe consciously and feel the air come in and go out. Burn a red candle and dance to your own music. If you don't dance, do calisthenics, anything, just to get active and move. As the candle burns give it your anger and frustrations. Feel your body working, the blood flowing, and create energy with your movement.

Estelle Daniels

October 3

The Spill-it Spell for Shy People

If you've ever found yourself tongue-tied in front of a stranger, or shy and embarrassed in a group, try the following spell. First, carry a tiger's-eye gemstone—a stone of strength and confidence—in your pocket and hold it. Then, tighten and release your abdominal muscles several times, slowly, to help reduce stage fright. As you breathe, focus on relaxing through your slow exhalations. Smile at someone in the group you like, or think you could like, and see if you don't get a smile back. Finally, admit how you feel by saying: "For some reason I always feel nervous in front of a group I don't know well. Have you ever felt that way?" If all else fails, talk about pets. Most people have or have had a pet and love animals. Get them started on Fluffy or Rex and the conversation's in the bag.

Amber K

4 October

Libra Energy Spell

Painting is used in this spell to empower a desire or need. First, paint the symbols of Venus (♀) and Libra (♎) on a piece of canvas or paper. Spend as much time working on the painting as you like. The idea is not to represent the desire perfectly, but to imbue the canvas with emotions that reflect on your desire. If you begin to worry or allow your mind to wander into negativity, stop. Come back to the work when you have cleansed the impure emotions from your mind. Burning a pleasing incense or listening to music while painting helps to keep a positive mood. Add spirals that begin from the outside and move to the center of the canvas while concentrating on your desires. When you are finished with the painting, hold your hands over the work and state your needs one last time.

Silver RavenWolf

October 5

Ring of Love Spell

You can attract the person you want to marry by wearing a love ring on the third finger of your left hand. To start, use your lover's Sun sign to acquire the stone from this list: Aries, bloodstone; Taurus, sapphire; Gemini, agate; Cancer, emerald; Leo, onyx; Virgo, carnelian; Libra, peridot; Scorpio, aquamarine; Sagittarius, topaz; Capricorn, ruby; Aquarius, garnet; Pisces, amethyst. Bring the stone to a jeweler and have it set into a gold band; then note the changes that occur in the relationship when you begin wearing it. If the stone changes the wearer into the kind of person who can attract and hold a love interest, then it will bring the relationship to you. If the band hurts or the stone falls out, the relationship will be difficult. If the ring fits perfectly and stays put, expect your lover to wind rings of love around you!

Marguerite Elsbeth

6 October

Music Spell

The following spell works best with classical music, though you may choose any music that deeply moves you. On a quiet evening alone, dress in a magical way and set up your stereo behind your altar. On the altar place pictures and symbols of the things you desire and need, then settle down into a comfortable position before the altar and fix your attention on the symbols of your desires. Start the music, and allow yourself to be swept along with it for some time—perhaps forty-five minutes or so—as you concentrate totally on your goal. Afterward, have a cup of coffee or something to eat.

Ed Fitch

October 7

Life-Everlasting Longevity Spell

To have a long life, with minimal illness, keep the life-everlasting plant *(Gnaphalium polycephalum)* in the living areas of your home. Even if you have suffered illness, bringing this plant into the house will help restore youth and vigor. Every morning, look at your life-everlasting plant and say: "Illness flee, and pain be gone. The life I live, may it be long."

Verna Gates

8 October

Home Protection Spell

To cast a spell to protect your home, during the waxing Moon and during the third hour after sunset pick a few stems of any combination of the following herbs: dill, fennel, marjoram, mint, mustard, mullein, rosemary, rue (if you are not allergic), white heather, woodruff, and yarrow. Tie small bundles of these herbs together with red thread and place on an altar. Touch the bundles with a ritual knife, saying: "I conjure thee, protective herbs, on this day and in this hour of Mars, to be a protection and safeguard against all adversity and evil. Protect well this house and all who dwell within. As I will, so mote it be!" Hang one bundle in each room of your home.

Ann Moura

October 9

Purification Spell for Air

If you need to get a message through to someone, force an issue, garner some added intelligence, or wish a friend health and happiness, air energy can push your spellwork to a speedy conclusion. Use the following incantation for area purification, the cleansing and blessing of supplies, or to invoke air energy into your magic circle: "Air flows pure. Spirit unbound. Inspiration! Sky to ground! Realize love with this sound." (Ring a bell seven times.) For an extra bit of punch, carve the air signs of the Zodiac—Gemini, Libra, and Aquarius—onto the candle color of your choice and burn during the ritual or spell casting, always asking for assistance from the element of air.

Silver RavenWolf

10 October

Malachite Amulet for Safe Travel

Malachite is a semiprecious gemstone with bands of lighter and darker green. To make a safe-travel amulet, obtain a piece of tumble-polished malachite from a rock shop, or an inset piece with malachite from a jewelry shop. To charge the amulet, stand with it cupped in your hands, then ground and center yourself. Achieve a mental state of alertness similar to the state you want to be in when driving your car. Breathe energy into the stone and speak in a strong decisive voice: "Safely go by foot and air; safely go by road and sea. Safely go ere I get there. As I will, so mote it be!" Carry the stone where you can see or feel it as you travel. In your car, affix it to the dashboard or suspend it from the rearview mirror. If you are using malachite jewelry, simply wear it until you arrive at your destination.

Amber K

Walnut Charms for Prosperity

For a prosperity spell, gather nine walnuts, nine old silver "Mercury" dimes (these have no copper in them and can be purchased at a coin store), nine whole cloves, nine crumbled cinnamon sticks, and some mustard seeds and bay laurel leaves. To start, carefully open the walnuts and clean out the shells. In each half shell, place one whole clove, some crumbled cinnamon stick and bay laurel, eighteen mustard seeds, and one dime. During a Full Moon, let moonlight shine on the contents in their shells, and feel the energy entering the coins and herbs. After meditating on this, take Super Glue and seal the two halves of each walnut together, taking care not to spill the contents. Paint the walnuts with gold metallic paint and leave on your altar. Take a walnut with you when you need a charge of prosperity.

Lori Bruno

12 October

The Mirror Image

For this love spell using image magic you will need a small mirrored surface that you have mentally cleansed and programmed to hold the image of your desire. During a waxing Moon, burn three pink or red candles while you anoint the rim of your mirror with a love oil such as vanilla, lavender, or clove. Project the image you wish to capture in your mirror onto its surface. If you do this while also seeing the reflection of the Moon, all the better. Cover the mirror until you are with the one you love, then contrive to capture your images in the glass at the same time. Cover it again until you are alone, and gaze into the mirror some time before dawn, "seeing" the captured image of your loved one. Cover it again and place it somewhere safe to bind your new love to you.

Edain McCoy

October 13

To Become Invisible

While there are many stories that involve magical cloaks and staves that render the hero invisible, in truth, the closest that many will ever come to true invisibility is when they journey into the astral. There is, however, a rite that has been used to endow the virtue of near invisibility. It enables one to walk into a room unobtrusively, unnoticed by all within. To begin, light a candle anointed with mystic veil oil. As it burns, anoint yourself with the oil as well, and go to the place where you wish to preserve your anonymity. You may find that even good friends will not notice as you quietly stride past. This rite can be combined with a specific purpose—for instance, those who wish to cross a border surreptitiously, or those who wish to gain insight by being unobtrusive. The possibilities are endless, and the results impressive.

Gwyndion O'Hara

14 October

Enhancing Courage Spell

To enhance your courage in a time of crisis, rub a red candle from the base to the top with rosemary essential oil during the first or eighth hour after sunrise or the third or tenth hour after sunset. Inscribe the candle with the following runic symbols: Lagu for protection and healing, Mann for the self, Ken for positive energy, Ur for personal strength, Daeg for a fresh start, Sigel for achievement and self-confidence, and Tyr for victory, courage, and success. Add your own astrological sign, saying: "Be these directed to me." Light the candle and wave your wand above it, and repeat: "I call on the energies of the ancient runes—earth, air, fire, water. As this candle melts, may these qualities enter into me; that as I will, so mote it be!" Let the candle burn down, then bury the remains in the ground or in a large potted plant.

Ann Moura

Spell to Secure Your Home

Protecting your homestead is a fundamental impulse. This energy can be used to build a psychic alarm system that will both alert you, and terrify a potential invader. To start, weave your mind from room to room as if your house were a loom and the thread of your thought an electric wire. Envisage your family and friends passing through your house with impunity, while those of negative intent are frazzled by your etheric network. As they struggle, their presence is conveyed to you. Should any enter intent on harm or wrongdoing, they will feel your power about them like a net, and you will intuitively sense their exact whereabouts. Frequently traverse your web, particularly before you fall asleep. Your domain soon will be avoided by those of negative intent.

Kala Trobe

16 October

Spell for Isis and Nephthys

Take black crepe streamers, available for Halloween decorations, and reverently loop them together to form a rough human shape. Place this on a table or altar, and think on your own sorrows and those of others. Say these or similar words: "Osiris is dead, nothing remains in this world but his wrappings. My dead, my Osiris, the sorrows of my world, all that remains are the empty wrappings which tie my heart. What they once contained has gone on to another dimension, where they cannot be seen. May the sorrow they leave behind no longer bind my heart. May only the light of their lives remain to be remembered." Burn the wrappings in the sink or in a heat-proof container. Watch the flames as they burn. When you at last look away, you will see only the afterimage of the light of the flames. Hold this in your heart.

deTraci Regula

A Spell for Untangling Communications

If you ever feel like communications with another person are tangled and going nowhere, you may wish to use this untangling spell. First, go off by yourself and take with you a piece of rope or cord at least twenty feet long. Throw it in the air repeatedly until it is thoroughly tangled. This represents your attempts at communication so far. Now sit down, center yourself, and breathe deeply. As you untangle the cord, ask yourself what single message you want to get across to the other party. Then ask yourself if you are really willing to hear the other's message. When you next talk to that person, take three short pieces of the cord along in your pocket. Use them to remember anything you've contributed to the misunderstanding, to restate the outcome you hope for, and to invite the other person to explain the position again.

Amber K

18 October

More Money Oil

This is an all-purpose oil to wear when job hunting, gambling, or making decisions about important purchases. Try to take a lighthearted approach to the matter, chanting: "Show me the money," while mixing the oil. Mix it on Thursday during the waxing Moon, when the Moon is in Jupiter, or during the hour of Jupiter. Blend equal parts prosperity (prosperidad) oil, money drawing (dinero rapido) oil, road opener (abre camino) oil, and success (suceso) oil. To charge the oil, pass it through the smoke of pine, frankincense, and myrrh incense. Use it to anoint your palms before work or a job interview; anoint your bank cards, lottery tickets, and such. Try to think up uses for it that will bring you money. And put a drop of the oil on each business letter you send.

Denise Dumars

Spell for a Stray Lover

To bring back a stray lover, during a waxing or Full Moon mix half a teaspoon of honey with ten drops of clove oil. Rub the mixture on six red candles, moving from the center to the base, then the center to the top of each in turn. As you do this, concentrate on your lover. Light the candles that call your lover from across the ether. Take a photo of the errant party and place in the center of the candles, saying: "I illuminate your mind." Very carefully anoint four fishing hooks with the oil mix. Think of each as luring your stray lover. Retrieve the photo from the center of the candles, and place a hook in the top right corner, and so on around the image, focusing on hooking them with your love from every angle. When finished, stash the photo with hooks still attached somewhere safe. Do not disturb unless you wish to release your fish.

Kala Trobe

20 October

Inviting in Your Ancestors

A good time to pay homage to your ancestors is just before Samhain. For this spell, gather at your altar or sacred space some black cloth, a black candle, a bowl of water, a feather, a citrine, amethyst or lapis lazuli crystal, and photos and mementos from your loved ones who have passed beyond. Place the black cloth on your altar or on the floor. Position the feather in the east, the candle in the south, the bowl of water in the west, and the crystal in the north. Arrange the photos and other objects in the middle as you chant or whisper: "May my loved ones touch me again—in the kiss of a breeze, in the light of candle flame, in the laughter of the rain, in the ground beneath my feet. Spirits of air, fire, water, earth, bring my loved ones close again." You may want to hold a photo or object and take time to feel the spirit of your loved one.

Sedwin

Day Lily Spell to Cure Sorrow

The day lily *(hemerocallis)* was grown in ancient China, but not in the flower garden. It was grown in the vegetable garden where it was prized for its delicate flavor. There is an added benefit to eating day lilies: It causes the kind of forgetfulness that cures all sorrow. To do this, pick the unopened buds, pinch off the ends, pull out the stamens and arrange them around your favorite dip for a blessing of an appetizer. Or, take buds and opened flowers, plucked-off stamens, and stir-fry them for just a couple of minutes until they are soft. If you like, sliver the part between root and green stem and add water chestnuts, serving over rice.

Verna Gates

22 October

New House Purification Spell

To purify your house, open the windows during a waning Moon or during the third or tenth hour after sunset. Light two red candles and set on the kitchen counter. Light a charcoal block and place in a cauldron between the candles. Grind equal parts bay leaf, yarrow flowers, rosemary leaves, St. John's Wort leaves, basil leaves, juniper berries, and mullein. Add the herbs to the glowing charcoal. Peel garlic cloves and place one in the center of each room. Carry the cauldron from room to room, censing each widdershins, then return it to the countertop between the candles. Vacate the house for thirteen minutes. Return and gather the garlic cloves without touching them, fasten in a plastic bag, and put outside in the trash. Close the windows, let the candles burn another hour, then snuff. Scatter the cooled incense remains out of doors. This spell is best done before occupancy.

Ann Moura

October 23

Warding Doors

Being a conscientious person, you lock your doors and check your windows at night to prevent someone getting in, but since there's been a rash of burglaries lately you're still nervous. After all, even though the practical precautions are taken care of you can always add some magical protection. So, for a lovely protection charm, take two pieces of beading wire and twist them to form the Eolh rune. Then, thread some amethyst or malachite chips onto the rune-shaped wire, and when you have covered the wire, cap the ends with enough hot glue to form a knob, preventing the chips from falling off. Affix this rune to your door and envision its protective energy keeping all negativity at bay.

Yasmine Galenorn

24 October

Blessing an Airliner

Before leaving on a journey by air, bless the plane in which you are traveling. Imagine yourself storing up thirteen or more breaths of life-force within yourself as you settle in your seat and fasten your seatbelt. Then breathe out the life-energy as you strongly imagine that you are fixing the power into critical parts of the aircraft—wings, engines, tail assembly, flight deck, and controls. You might wish to mentally draw a triple circle of protection around the entire airplane, and add a blessing: "May the protection of the Lord and the Lady be in and about this craft, that it may deliver us safely to our destination. May this craft always be a place of safety, serenity, and security for all who travel within. So mote it be!"

Ed Fitch

October 25

Counting Blessings Spell

When counting your blessings this year, add to your prosperity by using ritual at every step of the process. When cooking, add sage liberally to dressing. Spices like nutmeg, cloves, cinnamon, ginger, and allspice add to prosperity. Whenever adding magical ingredients to recipes, stir clockwise. Say to yourself: "As I stir, I increase prosperity, love, and harmony at home." Ginger-scented or bayberry candles decorate the table, as do gourds, autumn leaves, and perhaps pomegranates or red apples. Before everyone begins to eat, don't forget to add a prayer: "Dearest Pomona, harvest goddess, thank you for this bounteous harvest. Dearest Jupiter, god of prosperity, thank you for the means to purchase these fine foods. Dearest Juno, goddess of community, thank you for the strength to work toward our goals, and bless our family and friends this year."

Denise Dumars

26 October

The Enchanted Kiss

Fairy tales are strewn with tales of enchantment and curses made or broken by the power of a kiss. These days, a kiss can still be used to seal the interest of a new romantic partner. For this spell, get a new lipstick or lip balm and keep it with you all day so that it connects with your energy. In the evening put some cinnamon, vanilla, jasmine, or damiana into a glass of cold water. Twist out the lipstick or balm out as far your safely can and dip it into the mixture three times saying: "For my lips I make this spell; with one kiss our love will swell. Passion fired, our love to be; bound in charm between you and me." Do not eat or drink anything until you can kiss your new love interest.

Edain McCoy

Apple Peel Spell

This is a very old spell that is best used close to Halloween, or at the dark of the harvest Moon. First, peel an apple in one continuous piece. If you make a mistake and break the peel, finish peeling that apple, and try another one. (This is a good spell to try when you are baking pies.) Once you have accomplished your task, throw the apple peel over your left shoulder onto the kitchen floor. The peel will form the initial of the name of your future wedding mate.

Magenta Griffith

28 October

Changing a Dark Mood

If you find yourself caught in the midst of a dark mood that you can't shake, try this spell. While holding a cup filled with water, speak all the dark thoughts that come up into the water. Continue doing this until you can't think of anything more to say. Pour the water out into a river or onto some dirt, thus allowing the Earth to take your dark mood away. Then, holding a second cup of water, speak all your gratitudes. Start by thanking the Earth for taking your dark mood away. Continue until you cannot think of anything more to say. Then slowly drink the water, imaging the great things that you have spoken flowing into your life in abundance.

Therese Francis

October 29

Find Your Perfect Pet

It's Saturday, and the ASPCA is sponsoring pet adoptions. How do you choose your perfect pet? Try this technique. Sit in a comfortable place. Close your eyes and breathe deeply, exhaling completely each time until you feel deeply relaxed. Count from ten to one, then open your eyes. Rub your hands together quickly, then separate them. Repeat until you can feel the flow of energy even when the hands are separated. Practice while chanting, "Love flows between us." Now you are ready. At the pet adoption, approach your preferred species or breed. Do not try this on skittish or hostile animals. Once you find an amicable-seeming fuzzy friend, try the hand-rubbing technique. When separating your hands, place palms toward the animal and say: "Love flows between us." Watch the animals' responses. The one that responds most positively is the one for you!

Denise Dumars

30 October

Win at Sports Spell

For an edge over the competition in sports, during the second or ninth hours after sunrise, or the fourth or eleventh hours after sunset, inscribe a yellow candle with the runes Rad, Ken, Tyr, and Ur. Light dragon's blood incense, and say: "I call upon the power and energy of dragon's blood that I may be victorious!" Drop orris root into the candle, saying: "Let my competition not exceed me!" Drop in woodruff leaves, and say: "Let me overcome all obstacles!" Drop in bergamot leaves, and say: "Let my success be enhanced!" Raise energy then direct with wand into the candle flame, and chant:

> By root and by herb, by resin and light;
> The victory shall be mine by right!
> This spell is my bond, so mote it be!

Ann Moura

October 31

Halloween Spell

For many witches throughout the world, Halloween is an ideal time to magically do away with weaknesses. The Celts of old, for instance, on Samhain slaughtered all livestock that were too weak to live through the coming winter. Using a quill pen and dragon's blood ink, write upon a piece of parchment the weaknesses you wish to be rid of. As you concentrate on your intent, crumple up the paper in your "power hand" and toss it into a fire or set it ablaze by holding it above the flame of a black candle. Place it into a fireproof container such as a cast iron cauldron, and as the parchment burns away into ashes, so too shall your weaknesses be consumed by the flames of magic.

Gerina Dunwich

1 November

Spell for Prosperity

To promote prosperity, take a green, gold, or silver candle and anoint it with aromatic oils. Light the candle and work to pay bills, balance your checkbook, or review your budget. Ask yourself where you are wasting your resources. Is there anything—any expensive habits—you can get rid of to save a little money? As the candle burns, resolve to be a better money manager and envision yourself with a little more money at the end of the month. Little by little it soon mounts up.

Estelle Daniels

Sit Here, My Dear

If you are interested in someone romantically, make a small talisman by using a pink or red thread to bind love-inducing herbs such as myrtle, rue, apple blossom, mimosa, magnolia, rye, rosemary, and primrose in a small swatch of cheesecloth. As you tie the talisman, visualize it drawing to you the interest and attention of your romantic interest, and chant: "By my will this charm instill, the love in another that I will; when the power of this charm is set, may the flame of interest be lit." At the last possible moment, place the talisman under a place where your intended will sit, and wait for the charm to work its magic. One word of warning: Make sure the right person takes that seat or you could be for an interesting evening of unwanted adoration.

Edain McCoy

3 November

Kim's Spell

Remember that cat-spell in the old Kim Novak and Jimmy Stewart movie, *Bell, Book, and Candle*? It really works! To begin, light a candle or start a fire in the fireplace. Relax with your favorite pet, petting and talking as you do so. Then, humming a tune which has magical meaning to you, affix your eyes with your pet's. With your mind, send forth to your pet the image of the things you truly and honestly desire. The subconscious of your little friend will amplify and send forth your will and desire all the stronger. Afterwards, pet and cuddle your animal friend and offer some food.

Ed Fitch

Chicory Breaking Barriers Spell

If there is something that you need to retrieve or an obstacle you need to overcome, chicory (*Cichorium intybus*) provides you with the tools. Just break off the stems of chicory and rub the juice over your limbs while thinking of a barrier you want to break through. If you need to retrieve something, chicory can provide both invisibility and lock disposal. To craft the charm, the chicory root must be gathered in utter silence during Midsummer at one of the two high points of the clock, noon or midnight. Use a gold knife and chant: "As eyes glance my way, they see me not. They turn away." Use the empowered root to break the lock by holding it against the keyhole.

Verna Gates

5 November

A Knot Magic Spell for Finding Lost Objects

This powerful spell originated in Greece, and is used to locate lost objects. All you need is a handkerchief made of natural fabric, some soil, and your powers of concentration. To begin, picture the lost item in your mind. As you visualize the lost object, tie the handkerchief into a knot. Then take the knotted handkerchief out to your garden (apartment dwellers may use a potted plant) and press the knot into the soil while speaking these words: "Back to the earth, back to the ground. I won't untie you until you are found." Leave the handkerchief undisturbed until you find the lost item. When it is found, give thanks and untie the knot. Launder the handkerchief; put it away in a safe place to use again as needed.

Jim Weaver

November 6

Scorpio Energy Spell

Although Scorpio is a water sign, it carries the energy of the fire down-below. To tap into this energy, on a Tuesday or Saturday fill an old cooking pot with water, and add three pieces of jet, ½ teaspoon of angelica, ½ teaspoon of elder tree leaves, and one teaspoon of lemon juice. On a piece of paper outline the problem and the resolution needed. Draw the sigils for Pluto (♇) and Scorpio (♏) over the pot and at the top and bottom of your paper. Fold the paper into a small triangle. Bring the mixture to a boil and add the paper triangle, visualizing a positive outcome. Boil the water out of the mixture, being careful to avoid creating a hazard. Turn off the burner, and allow the pot to cool. Scrape the contents into a bowl, and empty the bowl at a crossroads at midnight.

Silver RavenWolf

7 November

Circle of Protection Spell for Safe Travel by Car

Speak this spell after you and your passengers have buckled your seat belts before a trip in your car:

> Mercury and Iris, winged god and rainbow goddess,
> Bless and protect this car and all of its parts,
> Its hood and engine, its tires and brakes.
> Keep the birds and beasts and other critters at a safe distance,
> Make me a skilled and careful driver,
> And grant that we may safely reach our destination.
> Circle of protection, one, two, three!

As you speak, visualize three circles of blue light surrounding your vehicle and traveling with it. Now act in accord by keeping your mind on your driving and your hands on the steering wheel.

Amber K

Money and Timing Ritual

We all have times when the checkbook won't balance; money due us isn't arriving, but the bills sure are! Try this emergency finance-boosting ritual for those times when money is running out. Take three peppercorns, or three drops of black pepper essential oil, and place them in a clear ceramic or Pyrex cup. Now add a pinch of cinnamon, ginger, or other "hot" money spice. Take off your watch—the one you wear everyday—and set it before the cup. Put the teakettle on. As you're waiting for the water to boil, chant: "Time, time, plenty of time, money arrives in plenty of time." When the water boils, fill the cup. Inhale the steam from the cup, and if your watch is water-resistant pass it through the steam as well. Repeat as necessary to encourage swift remuneration.

Denise Dumars

9 November

Love in a Tea Cup

To cast a potent love spell, during a waxing Moon
make a cup of herbal tea by placing in two mugs
a heaping teaspoon of tea made from crushed
and blended hyacinth, peppermint, grated lemon
peel, and clove. Add a sprinkle of cinnamon or
nutmeg and a few drops of vanilla extract, and fill
the mugs with boiling water. Place the two mugs
side-by-side, and stir clockwise while switching
back and forth between mugs. Keep the liquid in
both in constant motion as you chant: "By this
brew, three times three, a drink for two I wish
with thee. When my face you look and see, love
will come forever to be." As you share this with
the person whose heart you wish to capture,
make sure you are the first person he or she sees
after you both sip the shared drink.

Edain McCoy

Tarot Card Changing Spell

Sometimes in a tarot reading, you see a card whose appearance or position worries you. Here is a spell to alter one card in a spread. This provides magical support for whatever practical action you intend to take to change the outcome of events. To begin, light a candle of suitable color (green for money, brown for security, and so on) and set it nearby. Concentrate on the change you want to make, and recite this charm: "Here the paths are spread before me, as the fates have decreed. Now I choose a different way from the one I have laid, and this will change my destiny. As I will, so mote it be!" Change the card's position or replace it with another. Recite the charm again, pouring all your emotion into it. Then leave the cards alone; let the candle burn in a safe place, and pick everything up after it goes out.

Elizabeth Barrette

11 November

Spell Against Infections and Viruses

Nobody is invulnerable, but this spell will help protect against pesky infections spread by ailing colleagues. Hold some salt skyward, saying: "Angelic beings, bless this salt, that it may protect me against ailments." Visualize it glowing bright blue-white, then place it in a black silk pouch. Hold the charcoal and say: "Into this substance is illness absorbed." Place it in another black silk pouch. Carry both with you always. When sneezed at or breathed upon, subtly throw a little salt between you and the contagious party. Imagine any infections in your proximity repelled by your colored salt aura and being drawn in and earthed by the charcoal. Once a month, bury or burn the old charcoal and replace with fresh. This dual action should ensure against unnecessary illnesses.

Kala Trobe

November 12

Find a Lost Object

If you've lost something and have nowhere else
to look, hold something similar to the lost object
and say: "If I were a wallet (or other missing object), where would I hide?" Then go to wherever
your hand moves you.

Therese Francis

13 November

A Spell Against Thieves

To cast a spell of protection against thieves, first hang a painting or a photograph of eyes (the bigger the better) in a prominent place in your place of business. Then, mount two quartz crystals behind the eyeballs, and charge them with energy during the waxing Moon. Post this sign near the merchandise that tends to walk out unpaid for most often, and say: "Who steals a thing from here, no matter how small, walks out with a weight that's huge. The price is high to you though you think it's free; for you leave behind your honor and pride and honesty." Finally, when you see someone suspicious enter the shop, imagine that you are Mercury, god of thieves, and look at them until they see you looking.

Ed Fitch

November 14

The Slow Glass Spell

When someone yells at you, or asks you a question you're not prepared for, you can become easily flustered. This is the perfect time to shut up and try the Slow Glass Spell. The idea comes from a science fiction novel about a kind of glass that allows light to pass through only very slowly. An image entering one side wouldn't be seen on the other until many minutes, or even years, have passed. Imagine, therefore, a thick plate of slow glass between you and the other party. Time moves normally on the opposite side, but the glass makes time move slowly on your side. The other person's words and actions come through at a snail's pace, so impatience, thoughtlessness, harshness, and so on hardly pass through at all. You have all the time in the world to make a response.

Amber K

15 November

Jupiter Money Spell

If your bills have grown lately, or if you have a big balloon payment coming due, take a brown or black balloon. Hold it in your hand and contemplate your financial pressures. Inflate it, sending into it all of your anxiety over finances, saying: "I'm blowing away my money troubles today!" in between breaths. Then, tie it somewhere you can see it everyday. As the balloon deflates, your anxiety over finances will diminish through paid bills and unexpected extra money. And if your problems are too intense to wait for the balloon to deflate, fill the balloon, take it outside, then vigorously pop it with a pin.

deTraci Regula

One Whale of a Love Spell

If you are interested in hooking a big one, begin by taking some ambergris (for the whale's sake, you may use a synthetic version), a cassette tape of whale calls, and some shiny silver coins to the nearest natural body of water. Sit on the shore, and play the tape. Hold the ambergris and coins in your right hand while you talk to the water, telling it of your love for this special person. Now, remain silent, focusing your gaze on the water. When you see tiny stars dancing on the surface, anoint the coins with some of the ambergris and toss them into the water. Dab the remaining ambergris on your body, and get ready to sample the catch of the day.

Marguerite Elsbeth

17 November

Giving Thanks Blessing

Around the world, people in many cultures give thanks for the food they eat every day. This is a wonderful custom that fits in with all Pagan traditions. This nondenominational thanksgiving blessing can be used to give thanks:

Nuts and berries, roots and leaves,
Bounty born of all that lives,
Fruit in trees and grain in sheaves;
Praise for all the good Earth gives!

Tailor this for your own religion by substituting any two-syllable name or title for "good Earth" or any one-syllable term for "Earth."

Elizabeth Barrette

Tarot Spell for Clarity

Begin this clarifying spell with an oil that is not too floral or spicy, and anoint a pale blue candle from the center outward, concentrating on your situation. In a quiet place, where you won't be interrupted, light the candle. Hold in your hand the Ace of Cups card from your favorite tarot deck. State your situation in a short precise sentence, and concentrate on the water in the card. Follow your breath. The water will begin to move. Shapes may form, either as answers to your question, or as an entity who rises out of the water to speak with you. Do this for fifteen minutes a day until the candle burns out. You will know what you need to do by then.

Cerridwen Iris Shea

19 November

Old-Movie Magic

If you or a close friend needs healing, concentrate strongly on the illness, then rent a really funny old movie—such as ones with the Marx Brothers, Laurel & Hardy, or Bob Hope. Enjoy the film, laugh a lot, and as you laugh, always keep in mind the healing that you wish to have happen.

Ed Fitch

November 20

Warrior's Spell

During the third or tenth hour after sunset, take one mandrake or bronze fennel root, and pass it through incense smoke and a candle flame. Then sprinkle with water and salt, saying: "I consecrate this root by the powers of the elementals that it may be cleansed and purified to aid in my work." Set the root on a pentacle, saying: "Little man, listen to me. I'll dress thee and keep thee in my company, that thou turn aside harm from my fighting man, that he return safely as soon as he can." Wrap the root in red cotton yarn. Raise energy and direct it into the rootman, saying: "In the eye of Mars, by the fires of fury, let my warrior be steadfast, safe-kept, and victorious." Wrap the root in a red cloth and hide in a safe place. Keep it there until the warrior returns, then unbind the root and bury it.

Ann Moura

21 November

Choosing an Essay Topic Spell

If you're a student and you can't decide what to write a paper on, you might try using bibliomancy or map divining to help you choose. To begin, close your eyes, and open a relevant book at random. Put your finger on the page you have opened to, and open your eyes. The sentence or paragraph should give you an idea for a subject. For a history or geography paper, get out a map relevant to the coursework. If you don't own a dowsing pendulum, make one by tying a ring on a heavy thread about twelve to fifteen inches long. Hold the thread in your thumb and forefinger on your non-dominant hand, and dangle this over the map. Slowly move the pendulum over the map, stopping to let it come to rest. At some point, the pendulum will refuse to rest, probably making circles in the air. This should suggest a topic for your paper.

Magenta Griffith

November 22

Wishbone Spells

To find out which of two unmarried maidens will be the first to marry, have each take hold of the same wishbone and together break it into two pieces while saying: "Bone, I wish the future read. Who shall be the first to wed?" The girl who receives the bigger of the two pieces will walk down the aisle before the other. This old method of marriage divination is English in origin and dates back at least to the Middle Ages. Deriving from it is our popular custom of two persons making a wish while breaking a wishbone apart.

Gerina Dunwich

23 November

Heart's Ease Tarot Spell

To ease your hurting heart, place the Ace of Cups, the Four of Swords, and the World cards from your favorite tarot deck on a blue cloth. Place a white jar candle, a hematite stone, and some rosemary incense around the cards. Turn on some soothing music, and light the incense and the candle, chanting, "Safe, soft, simple," over and over until you feel sleepy. Lie down and nap for a couple of hours. Upon awakening, you will feel refreshed and confident that healing has begun. Jot down any dreams or information you received during the nap. Do this once or twice a week until healed.

Cerridwen Iris Shea

November 24

Sea-Life Divination

As you look out at the moonlit ocean at night from a high point of land, look for areas on the ocean that might seem a bit brighter than normal. Try to imagine why these concentrations of power are present. Quite likely the light is due to the presence of one or more water elementals. Gaze softly out at the light and eventually visions will come to you.

Ed Fitch

25 November

Preparing for Winter's Inward Journey

To prepare for the season of cold, in early winter at your favorite outdoor place gather three acorns, a white-handled knife, and some blue corn meal. Sprinkle a light dusting of corn meal on the ground, then cup the acorns in both hands and raise them to the sky, saying: "Mother of grain create sacred space. Lord of trees protect this place. Prepare me for winter's cold and snow, and send me a vision of where I must go. By the power of three, so mote it be." Using the knife, loosen a small patch of soil, then gently bury one of the acorns. Leave a second acorn as an offering. Keep the third on your altar or special place as you meditate or do a solo ritual through the winter.

Sedwin

November 26

Room Cleansing Spell

To cleanse a room, during the eighth hour after sunrise or the third hour after sunset place the following items on a tray: one sprig of white heather, one lit white candle in a holder, lit frank-incense in a holder, and a bowl of blessed water (salted and consecrated). Take the candle and the incense and walk around the interior of the room saying: "By fire and flame, by smoke and scent, I drive from this room all chaos and dissent." Asperse the water around the room using the sprig, sprinkling the baseboards, walls, cornices, and floor saying: "By water and salt, by herb and flower, peace and contentment return in this hour." Take the tray out of doors and say: "Follow the light, follow the scent. Into the earth and into the air, energies gathered here I now vent." Blow out the candle, and bury the incense, laying the sprig and pouring the water on top.

Ann Moura

27 November

Celtic Cross Spell

Making the sign of the cross acts as a protective spell, even for non-Christians, because it uses the powers of the four elements to act as a shield and barrier. As a variation of this gesture, you can draw a Celtic cross over your solar plexus—bad energy often goes straight to the stomach—when you have to deal with hostile people. To effect the spell, draw your fingers across your upper and lower abdomen to make an equal-armed cross. Repeat this motion several times, while visualizing a shield of protective energy building in front of you. Then, rub your palm around the area in a circular motion until you feel more relaxed. If you have to confront negativity on a regular basis, hang a Celtic cross on a very long cord, and wear it beneath your shirt, positioned about your navel.

Janina Renée

Tarot Travel Spell

Set out the Six of Swords, the Fool, and the Three of Cups cards from your favorite tarot deck left to right in front of you. Place the first of three stones you feel strongly connected to on the Six of Swords card, saying: "For safe travel." Place the second stone on the Fool, saying: "For a mind and heart open to adventure." Place the third stone on the Three of Cups, saying: "For a celebratory homecoming." Leave them to charge overnight in the moonlight. The next morning, cleanse the cards and return them to the pack. Place the stones in the bag and take the bag with you on your trip.

Cerridwen Iris Shea

29 November

An Appalachian Money Ritual

According to an old prosperity ritual from Appalachia, you should select a night between the New and Full Moon to hide a one-dollar bill outside your front door without telling anyone. Visualize the amount of your money growing. Early the next morning remove the dollar from the hiding place and put it in your pocket. Carry it with you all day and don't spend any money for the next twenty-four hour period. This ritual ensures money will keep coming into your life and that you will hang onto it. A good time to perform this ritual is New Year's Eve. In this way, you will attract money to yourself during the coming year.

Jim Weaver

November 30

Spell for Making a Wish

For a spell for making a wish, get two different colored candles and light them. Write down your wish, but also speak it out loud. Tell the candles and the cosmos what you want and why you want, need, and deserve it. Create a simple affirmation that you can chant as you burn the paper and let the smoke carry your wish to heaven.

Estelle Daniels

1 December

Tarot Harmony Spell

For this spell, light a white candle, and say: "For purity." Light a blue candle, and say: "For harmony." Light a peach one, and say: "For affection." Watch the candlelight, following your breath, and place the Three of Cups card from your favorite tarot deck before the candles. Stare into the card, imagining harmony among the parties involved, or harmony and celebration in your life in general. Repeat "Purity, harmony, affection" nine times. Imagine passing a chalice around a group, everyone sharing, then drinking the contents yourself. Extinguish the candles and walk away. Do this each day until the candles burn down.

Cerridwen Iris Shea

December 2

Candle Spell

To fulfill all your wishes, in the evening light five
candles of the color that symbolizes each thing
you wish. Concentrate deeply on what you desire, then blow out the candles. Try not to think
about the subject of your magic for the rest of the
evening. Children especially seem to like this spell.

Ed Fitch

3 December

Untangling Spell

Get nine ribbons, cords, or lengths of yarn, each in a different color. Place them on a cloth and mix them up. Take a deep breath and say: "Lachesis, Clotho, Atropos, Fates Three, help me to unravel this mystery. As I organize these strands in a row, may my life make sense to know." Untangle all nine threads and place them in a row. Take three, knot them off, and braid them. Repeat with three more, then three more. You should end up with three braided cords. Braid these cords together and carry it with you. Your answers will come in surprising and often beautiful ways.

Cerridwen Iris Shea

December 4

Power Raising Spell

Often, practitioners of magic need to raise power. You may want to do this inside a cast circle during a ritual, or while meditating or walking outside. It requires no props or material components, and no special preparation. It is simply an entreaty to the gods and the universe at large to dispense power in your direction. Repeat this simple chant over and over again until you have as much energy as you need:

> Give me, O give me
> A touch of magic
> A kiss of magic
> The bliss of magic!

You can use this spell to increase the general amount of magic in your life, but be careful what you wish for, because you're likely to get it.

Elizabeth Barrette

5 December

A Spell for a Safe Trip

To help you return home safely from a trip place a pinch of lavender, a pinch of mint, and one penny on a white handkerchief, and tie up this bundle with a yellow ribbon. Place this magical bundle beneath your pillow just before leaving home and say: "If I travel near or travel far, protect me. If I roam in plane, train, boat, or car, I will return safely home." After returning home give thanks and keep the little bundle in a safe place, then recharge it before traveling again with the same words.

Jim Weaver

Cooking for Prosperity Spell

To promote prosperity from the kitchen, keep a good countenance whenever you cook food and transfer good wishes to the food. Your stove is the sacred hearth. Your wooden spoon is a magical wand. Be careful never to cook in anger. Always stir the pot with a clockwise motion, and wish health, wealth, and joy upon all who will eat the food. You may say this from time to time as you cook:

> The gods do bless you,
> when you give with love.
> This is the greatest spell,
> which encompasses all.

Lori Bruno

7 December

Love Is in the Air Spell

To create a potent perfume that will draw the romantic attention of the opposite sex, during a Full Moon mix the following oils or herbs in an olive or almond oil base in proportions pleasing to both your nose and magical senses. For women seeking men: vanilla extract or oil, clove oil, rose oil, and willow bark. For men seeking women: musk oil, orange or lime oil, nutmeg oil, and dried yarrow. Apply the perfume to chakra or pulse points before going out to meet your prospective lovers.

Edain McCoy

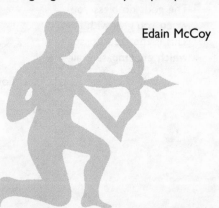

December 8

Sagittarius Energy Spell

If you need to expand your horizons, tap into Sagittarian energies by popping one bag of unbuttered popcorn. As the kernels expand, imagine the opportunities you wish drawing toward you. String the popcorn and some holly leaves on a sturdy thread. The longer the garland, the better. As you string each piece, concentrate on your desire. Knot the thread to finish the garland, stating your intention aloud. Hold your hands over your project, again thinking of your intention. Make the sign of Jupiter ($\mathrm{2\!\!\!/}$) and the sign of Sagittarius ($\nearrow$) in the air over your work. Place the garland on your altar until your wish has been granted. Then, burn the garland outside, thanking the spirit for the gifts you have received. Note: You can also hang the garland on your Yule tree or over a doorway for the holiday season.

Silver RavenWolf

9 December

Strength for Surgery Spell

Before surgery you may cast this spell during the third hour after sunrise or the first or eighth hour after sunset. Begin by speaking: "On this day of great energy, in this hour of self-preservation, I call upon the ruling powers and the elementals to aid me." Anoint two light blue votive candles with cypress essential oil. Inscribe on one the runic symbol Beorc, the goddess; on the other, Os, the god. Set the candles on the altar and light, saying: "I call upon the Lady and the Lord to stand by me. Let the power of thy love and thy protection surround me, that this surgery be successful and I gain good health." Drop rosemary and St. John's Wort leaves into the flames. Say: "By the power of the Lady and the Lord, by herb and by light, let ill health take flight! So mote it be!" Let the candles burn down. Bury the remains.

Ann Moura

The Rebirth of Light Spell

As the Winter Solstice approaches, a major theme in world magic is luring back the power of light in its many forms. To bring light back into your life, use either a Hanukkah menorah or nine taper candles, and, while in complete darkness, light them one at a time saying the following:

1) A hint of light in darkness glows,
2) Waxing slowly, the light, it grows,
3) The cover of darkness shall banished be
4) As in time each season must fade and flee.
5) A balance is found in dark and light,
6) But now the victor is the Sun God's might.
7) Sacred flame that burns and sizzles bright
8) Burn in me as darkness bows to light.
9) The season turns yet once again; I open the portal to let light in.

Edain McCoy

11 December

Evil Eye Spell

In folkloric societies, the term "evil eye" refers to the transfer of negative energy that can occur when one person looks upon another with a jealous heart. Many of us who work in modern society may experience a sort of evil eye effect when, in the course of doing our jobs, we anger other people. Charms against the evil eye can be helpful in these cases. Consider getting a traditional amulet that includes the beads with circular designs known as "eye beads," though you many use any shiny bead for this purpose. If permissible, hang beads on strings about your work place: attached to drawer handles, the branches of plants, and so on to create a feng shui effect against angry glances. Or you may consider wearing such a bead on a string around your wrist or neck as you work.

Janina Renée

December 12

Travel Protection Sachet

To protect yourself during travel, combine equal amounts of mustard seed, comfrey, Irish moss, and kelp (also known as bladderwrack). Tie these up in a white or yellow cloth and carry with you when you travel. You may even choose to tuck one into each of your suitcases and garment bags.

Scott Cunningham

13 December

Victory in Vegas

Here are some suggestions to aid gamblers in Las Vegas or other gaming meccas. Charms: Good-luck charms should be carried in a green pouch; charms include buckeyes, lodestones, whole nutmegs, small horseshoe-shaped magnets, or a piece of High John the Conqueror root. Gambling oils: The best commercial one I've found is Anna Riva's Haitian Gamblers' Oil, but you can also make your own, blending cypress, basil, and rosemary oils and adding rosemary needles, mint or basil leaves, or pine needles. Rub on palms and on money you gamble with. Beating the odds: Since odds are on the house, it's to your advantage to think positively about the casino as you enter. Smile, tip well, be friendly, and manifest a positive aura. If you're really good at this, you may earn unexpected "comps" such as free meals, drinks, and tickets just by lending a positive atmosphere to the place!

Denise Dumars

Love Sigil Spell

In front of an image of Venus or Aphrodite and a cup of water, place twelve copper or silver coins in the form of the goddess's sigil—a circle balanced on top of an equal-armed cross. Start with the right side of the circle, bringing the divine energy down as you arrange the earth cross, then go the left, ascending side of the crowning. Say these words as you place each coin: "I ask you, great goddess of love, to look upon me kindly from above; let your love of greatest worth find me here and now." Leave the sigil set up until love enters your life; if it is a love you want to endure, glue the coins to a board and place behind your image of Aphrodite-Venus.

deTraci Regula

15 December

Saturn Tarot Spell

To seek the guidance of Saturn, take the Major Arcana cards from your tarot deck. Shuffle and then hold them in your hands. Close your eyes, and meditate on Saturn the planet, and its rings. Take in energy as you inhale; ground yourself as you exhale. Now open your eyes, and turn over the first card in the deck. If the card is Strength, the Star, the Hierophant, or the High Priestess, your influence is strong today. Go get 'em! If the card is Death, the Devil, the Hanged Man, or the Tower, Saturn is trying to contact you. Ask him what he has to tell you. Now turn over two more cards. One of the two should have a special meaning for you. Try this spell over a period of weeks. It will calm and center you, and give you some amount of insight.

Denise Dumars

December 16

Health Spell

To promote good health, during the seventh hour after sunrise grind in a mortar two teaspoons lavender flower and one teaspoon each of thyme, allspice, coriander seed, and willow leaf, saying: "I charge you by the Sun and the Moon, on this day of high energy and in this hour of healing, to release your powers into my work!" Rub peppermint oil on a blue votive candle and inscribe with these symbols, saying: "Jupiter for health, Beorc for the Goddess, Water for fluids, Tyr for victory, Os for the God, and Sigel to direct the healing energy." Light the candle in a cauldron. Add the herbal mixture, and say: "I call upon the divine to hasten my healing, bringing victory over the watery confusion in my body; with healing herbal energies released to my aid, cast aside my sickly imbalance I bid thee. So mote it be!" Burn one hour, snuff, and bury the remains.

Ann Moura

17 December

Come-Set-a-Spell

If you can't get your child to hold still and talk to you, go to the kitchen and begin a project that occupies your hands—like decorating holiday cookies. When your child comes to the kitchen, whisper: "If it be the Lady's (or Lord's) will, talk to me, come set a spell. Ears to hear and lips to speak, some time with you is all I seek." Then invite your child to help with the project. As she works, match the rhythm of your breathing to hers, then gradually slow it down so she will unconsciously match you. When you are both relaxed, ask a simple question such as what kind of nose she'd like on the snowman cookies. Gradually you may turn to more thoughtful questions: "What is your favorite part of the holidays?" or "How do you feel when you give someone a present?" And behold: Quality time with your child.

Amber K

Good Hunting Spell

During the third hour after sunset on the day before hunting, inscribe a red candle with the runic symbols Rad, Tyr, and Eohl, and light it. Light patchouli incense, and say: "Let this earthy scent attune me with Herne the Hunter, the bounty of the Earth, and the natural forces of life's cycles." Drop the following herbs into the candle, speaking after each. Star anise: "I call upon the spirits of hunter ancestors to aid me in my hunt tomorrow." Bergamot leaves: "I call upon the power of bergamot to bring me success tomorrow." Artemesia leaves: "I call on the Lady of the Hunt to bring me success in my endeavors tomorrow." Red dianthus (carnation) petals: "I honor the blood of the animal I seek; life unto life, I hunt what I eat. The cycles we share flow ever eternal; hunters and hunted, revered and fraternal."

Ann Moura

19 December

Photo Power Spell

To display a photo or other type of picture is an act of magic, for photographs preserve the power of memory. The photos you keep affirm your connection with people, places, or the person you were at some time in the past, and every time you view these images, the connections are reactivated. To preserve the magical moment captured in a photo or to invoke the power of an ideal expressed in a picture, write the following words on the back of the image, or on a separate piece of paper to be inserted into the frame behind it: "Time through time, bid time return. Likeness of life, through power of art, eternally young." To further fix this spell, you can also draw symbols such as hearts, flowers, and the infinity symbol, or attach colorful stickers, to the back of the picture or paper.

Janina Renée

December 20

Money Soup

This money soup can be made on New Year's Eve, or at any time, to attract money during the next year. Remove the silver object before eating the soup.

    1 coin or small silver object
    2 cups water
    1½ tablespoons butter
    1 large onion, minced
    1 small head green cabbage, shredded
    4 cups chicken stock
      Salt and pepper to taste

Boil the silver object to sterilize it. Melt the butter in a saucepan, add the onion and sauté till light brown. Add the cabbage and cook till tender. Toss in the silver object. Add chicken stock to vegetables and bring to a boil. Reduce heat and simmer fifteen minutes. Add salt and pepper to taste.

Scott Cunningham

21 December

Mistletoe Spell for Luck

With a consecrated ritual dagger, ceremonially cut a piece of mistletoe at sunrise on winter solstice. As you do this, recite thrice the following incantation: "Golden bough and Witch's broom, thy sacred names are spoken. By dagger's blade I conjure thee to see all bad luck broken. Harming none, this spell is done. By law of three, so mote it be!" Hang the white-berried plant over the front door of your house to bring good luck to all who dwell within. Mistletoe, which was sacred to the druids and used in their ancient fertility rites, is also said to possess the powers of healing and protection against evil, fire, illness, and bad luck.

Gerina Dunwich

December 22

Stone Divination

To discover something you want to know, stare at the gravel at a beach or river bank. Fix your mind on what you want to know, for perhaps a minute or so, as you stir the stones around with your right hand. Then look carefully for shapes on or among the stones, and interpret them. Based on what you want to know, what do they suggest to you?

Ed Fitch

23 December

Spell for Minor Ailments

Unnecessary minor ailments can be a bother. To avoid them, cast a circle and place yourself at the center. Light some jasmine oil or incense and visualize yourself rising into a violet, perfumed sphere. As you do so, let yourself feel emotional, and let your mind turn to nostalgia and to recollection. Before you drift away, light some frankincense oil or incense and rise up again until you reach a solar sphere, burning away trivial concerns and emotional bonds. Feel yourself purged of small-minded subjectivity as you abide here. Now light some sweet almond oil or incense. Rise up yet further, your personality stepping aside, your higher self stepping in. Attune yourself to this greater perspective. Ask that you remain in communion with this higher aspect of yourself. Unnecessary minor ailments should soon cease.

Kala Trobe

December 24

Spiritual Housecleaning Spell

The spiritual aspects of cleaning house are often used by the practitioner of Voodoo or Santeria. In botanicas, you will find many floorwashes, powders for sweeping, room sprays, and cleaning products with names like "House Blessing" and "Peaceful Home." These products are safe for home use and are recommended, but you can make your own. Put a few drops of essential oil of patchouli, cedarwood, and sandalwood into water. Cedarwood has the added benefit of re-pelling moths; cedar shavings can be hung in muslin bags in closets, or crushed cedar shavings can be spread on the carpeting before vacuum-ing. To attract blessings, mop or wash in a deosil fashion. To dispel negativity, clean in a widdershins direction. A general "House Blessing"—smudging of the house with cedar, sage, or sweetgrass—is recommended once a month as well.

Denise Dumars

25 December

Christmas Candle Spell

For good luck to smile upon you throughout the coming year, light a Yule-candle (a large mold-candle decked with evergreens) on Christmas or Christmas Eve. Recite the following incantation: "Candle of Yule with flame bright, you shall burn through this night. Bring us fortune and luck fair all through the coming year. So mote it be." Allow the Yule-candle to burn, undisturbed, until sunrise of December 26. A safe place to keep a burning Yule-candle overnight is either in the bathtub or kitchen sink. When time comes to put out the candle, extinguish the flame with a candle snuffer or by pinching it out between your moistened fingertips. Blowing it out, according to tradition, will cause all of your good luck to be scattered to the wind.

Gerina Dunwich

December 26

Kwanzaa begins

Bookstore Meditation

Did you ever wonder just which books, among all the many choices, are right for you? Try this and see. Start by wearing brown clothing, amber jewelry, and some amber perfume or a drop of one of Saturn's favorite oils—patchouli, sandalwood, cedarwood, or cypress. At the bookstore, meditate on the shelved books. Take in their titles and the colors of their covers. Take three deep breaths and listen to see if any books "call" to you. If so, buy one. If not, place your hands with palms toward the books. Move your hands slowly across the shelf. When your hand feels a warm spot, stop. Take the book off the shelf where you stopped. Continue the spell throughout any sections of the bookstore that interest you. You may find just the sort of book you've been looking for—or one you never expected to find at all!

Denise Dumars

27 December

Mandrake Money Spell

Mandrake (Mandragora officinarum), the most magical of herbs, can be used to gain money. First, activate the root by gathering it in a Full Moon with the point of a silver blade. Clean the root in spring water, and place it into a velvet-lined box. Put the box in an active part of the house, and leave it undisturbed for three days. On the third night, soak it in warm spring water overnight. The root is now ready for magic. Place the root back into the velvet-lined box, this time with silver coins. Lock the box and store it away. Your money will double.

Verna Gates

December 28

The Witch Bottle Spell

Witch bottles are popular in magic, and, though most often employed for protection, they can be effective talismans for drawing love into your life. In a clean glass jar place some or all of the following while visualizing love being drawn to your dwelling: spring water, a drop of your own blood, a strand of your own hair, vanilla extract, and a rose quartz stone. You may also use any form of coriander, cinnamon, hyacinth, licorice, yerba maté, rue, myrtle, lemon, lavender, jasmine, mastic, rose, peppermint, thyme, or plum. Drawings or other love talismans representing your goal of romance can also be included. During a Full Moon, bury the sealed bottle near an entryway to your home. It will work for a year and a day.

Edain McCoy

29 December

Good Day Tarot Spell

Place a white candle on your altar, and put the Fool card from your favorite tarot deck in front and slightly to the left of the candle. Put the World card in front and slightly to the right, and light the candle. Shuffle the tarot deck, thinking of wonderful things that you would like to happen today. Pull a card from the deck and place it between the Fool and the World cards. Meditate for a few moments on all the positive possibilities. Extinguish the candle, leave the cards on the altar, and make sure you smile at your reflection before leaving the house.

Cerridwen Iris Shea

Spell for Scrying

For a spell for seeing the future, light a white or
silver candle to do some scrying. Traditionally, you
use a bowl of water with the Full Moon reflected
in it, but you can use the reflection of a candle
flame instead. Let your thoughts drift as you gaze
at the light, and see what images you get. Write
them down and think about what they mean for
you. Think about a person or problem and try
again. See what insights or answers you are given.
There is a solution to every problem; allow your
inner mind to help you.

Estelle Daniels

31 December

New Year's Eve

This year, try writing your New Year's resolutions in dragon's blood ink on a square piece of parchment paper. This ink is traditionally used for spells involving strength and power. Then, upon the paper sprinkle a bit of dried mugwort, and roll it into a tube and secure it in the center with a red ribbon. Anoint a new white candle with bergamot oil as you state your resolutions aloud. Light the candle and then use its flame to set fire to the rolled-up parchment. Cast the parchment into a small cast iron cauldron (or other fireproof container) and thrice recite the following incantation: "To the flames my words are spoken as the newborn year unfolds. Resolutions be not broken, promises be upheld."

Gerina Dunwich

A Note on Magic

The spells in this calendar evoke everyday magic that is designed to improve our lives and homes. You needn't be an expert on magic to follow these simple rites and spells; as you will see, if you use these spells through the year, magic, once mastered, is easy to perform. The only advanced technique required of you is the art of visualization.

Visualization is an act of controlled imagination. If you can call up in your mind a picture of your best friend's face or a flag flapping in the breeze, you can visualize. In magic, visualizations are used to direct and control magical energies. Basically, the spell-caster creates a visual image of the spell's desired goal, whether it be perfect health, a safe house, or a protected pet.

Visualization is the basis of all good spells, and as such it is a tool that should be properly used. Visualization must be real in the mind of the spell-caster so that it allows him or her to raise, concentrate, and send forth energy to accomplish the spell.

Perhaps when visualizing, you'll find that you're doing everything right, but that you don't feel anything. This is common, for we haven't been trained to acknowledge—let alone utilize—our magical abilities. Keep practicing, however, for your spells can "take" even if you're not the most experienced natural magician.

Even when your spells are effective, magic won't usually sparkle before your very eyes. The test of magic's success is time, not immediate eye-popping results. But you can feel magic's energy for yourself by rubbing your palms together briskly for ten seconds, then holding them a few inches apart. Sense the energy passing through them, the warm tingle in your palms. This is the power raised and used in magic. It comes from within and is perfectly natural.

Have a magical year!

Glossary of Magical Terms

Altar: a low table that holds magical tools as a focus for spell workings.

Athame: a ritual knife used to direct personal power during workings or to symbolically draw diagrams in a spell. It is rarely, if ever, used for actual physical cutting.

Aura: an invisible energy field surrounding a person. The aura can change color depending upon the state of the individual.

Balefire: a fire lit for magical purposes, usually outdoors.

Casting a circle: the process of drawing a circle around oneself to seal out unfriendly influences and raise magical power. It is the first step in a spell.

Censer: an incense burner. Traditionally, a censer is a metal container, filled with incense, that is swung on the end of a chain.

Censing: the process of burning incense to spiritually cleanse an object.

Centering yourself: to prepare for a magical rite by calming and centering all of your personal energy.

Chakra: one of the seven centers of spiritual energy in the human body, according to the philosophy of yoga.

Charging: to infuse an object with magical power.

Circle of protection: a circle cast to protect oneself from unfriendly influences.

Crystals: quartz or other stones that store cleansing or protective energies.

Deosil: clockwise movement, symbolic of life and positive energies.

Deva: a divine being according to Hindu beliefs; a devil or evil spirit according to Zoroastrianism.

Direct/Retrograde: refers to the motions of the planets when seen from the Earth. A planet is "direct" when it appears to be moving forward from the point of view of a person on the Earth. It is "retrograde" when it appears to be moving backward.

Dowsing: to use a divining rod to search for a thing, usually water or minerals.

Dowsing pendulum: a long cord with a coin or gem at one end. The pattern of its swing is used to predict the future.

Dryad: a tree spirit or forest guardian.

Fey: an archaic term for a magical spirit or a fairylike being.

Gris-Gris: a small bag containing charms, herbs, stones, and other items to draw energy, luck, love, or prosperity to the wearer.

Needfire: a ceremonial fire kindled at dawn on major Wiccan holidays. It was traditionally used to light all other household fires.

Pentagram: a symbolically protective five-pointed star with one point upward.

Power hand: the dominant hand, the hand used most often.

Scry: to predict the future by gazing at or into an object such as a crystal ball or pool of water.

Second sight: the psychic power or ability to foresee the future.

Sigil: a personal seal or symbol.

Smudge/Smudge stick: to spiritually cleanse an object by waving incense over and around it. A smudge stick is a bundle of several incense sticks.

Wand: a stick or rod used for casting circles and as a focus for magical power.

Widdershins: counterclockwise movement, symbolic of negative magical purposes, and sometimes used to disperse negative energies.

Author Biographies

Amber K has been an ordained High Priestess of Wicca for almost twenty years. She is the author of the bestseller *True Magick,* and has traveled widely throughout the United States teaching the Craft.

Elizabeth Barrette is a regular contributor to a number of publications. Much of her involvement with the Pagan community takes place online, where she has helped build networking resources. Visit her own website at: http://www.worthlink.net/~ysabet/index.html.

Lori Bruno is a hereditary Sicilian Strega and founder of Our Lord and Lady of the Trinacrian Rose Coven in Massachusetts. She also helped create the Sacred Paths Alliance Network (SPAN), a charitable organization, and the Protective Organization of Witches & Earth Religions (POWER). Ms. Bruno is a descendant of Renaissance philosopher Giordano Bruno, who was condemned as a heretic and burned on February 17, 1600.

Scott Cunningham was a spiritual pioneer whose work lay the foundation for the noninstitutional growth of modern Wicca. Scott encouraged a new understanding of positive, nature-based magics using herbs, gems, and the elements. After a long illness, Scott passed from this life on March 28, 1993.

Reverend Estelle Daniels is a Pagan minister and member of the Wiccan Church of Minnesota. She is also a professional part-time astrologer and author of *Astrologickal Magick,* as well as a regular contributor to the Llewellyn annuals. Ms. Daniels visits festivals and gives workshops on astrology, Wicca, and other Pagan subjects.

Denise Dumars is a college English instructor and writer from Southern California. A member of the Temple of Isis in Los Angeles, she edited *Isis 2000: The Goddess in the New Aeon,* a collection of goddess poetry. Her magazine articles can be found in many journals.

Gerina Dunwich is a High Priestess of the Old Religion, astrologer, cat-lover, tarot reader, and author of such books as *Wicca Craft, Magick Potions,* and *The Wicca Source Book.* She founded the Pagan Poets Society and currently resides in California. Her website is http://www.geocities.com/ -Area51/Atlantis/1978.

Marguerite Elsbeth (a.k.a. Senihele and Sparrow Hawk) is a hereditary Sicilian Strega, and has Lenape (Delaware) Indian ancestry. She is a professional tarot and astrological reader, and a practitioner of Nativism (American Indian healing).

Marguerite has published numerous articles in Llewellyn's annuals, and is the author of several books. She resides in the Southwest.

Ed Fitch is a founder and major scholar of modern Paganism. Initiated into the Gardnerian Wicca during the mid-1960s, he has continually added to the background lore of Wicca and mainstream Paganism, and is considered to be one of the best and most influential writers of rituals in the U.S. today.

Therese Francis, Ph.D., is an herbalist, hands-on healer, counselor, and licensed minister. Dr. Francis gives workshops on shamanism and integrating the body, mind, heart, and spirit. She has written several books, including *20 Herbs to Take Outdoors* and *The Mercury Retrograde Book.*

Yasmine Galenorn is a writer and artist. She has been a Witch in the Craft since 1980 and is the author of several Llewellyn books. She also designed and runs the Galenorn En/Visions website at www.galenorn.com, and is the creator of the DarkMoon Rising tradition. She lives with her husband and cats in Washington State and can be reached at darkmoon@galenorn.com.

Verna Gates teaches folklore classes at the University of Alabama at Birmingham and was a writer for CNN. Her specialties are wildflowers, moonlore, and storytelling.

Magenta Griffith has been a Witch for twenty-five years, a High Priestess for twelve years, and a founding member of the coven Prodea. She presents workshops and classes at festivals and gatherings around the Midwest.

Edain McCoy has been a Witch since 1981. Today she is part of the Wittan Irish Pagan path and is a Priestess of Brighid. She is author of many books, and is currently at work on two new books on practical Witchcraft.

Dorothy Morrison is a Third Degree High Priestess of the Georgian Tradition and has taught the Craft to students in the U.S. and Australia. She is the author of several books, and currently lives in Maryland with her husband, Mark, and their black lab, Sadie Mae.

Ann Moura was raised in a family tradition of Green Witchcraft, which she has passed on to her children. She holds a graduate degree in history and is the author of several Llewellyn books. She is working on a book about components of magic. For recreation she tends her herb garden and travels the globe.

Gwydion O'Hara has been associated with Witchcraft in both the United States and Canada since the 1970s. He was initiated into an Alsacian tradition of Witchcraft, and has held that tradition closely ever since. In 1979, O'Hara gave up a successful corporate career to take on the obligations of Pagan priesthood full time. He has written several books.

Silver RavenWolf is the author of thirteen books on the magical sciences and religion. She is the Clan Head of the Black Forest Family, which currently has eighteen covens in thirteen states. Her primary interests are divinatory tools, astrology, hypnotherapy, and getting through life in a positive and productive way. She resides in southcentral Pennsylvania with her husband, four children, sheltie, and pet rat. Visit her website at: http://www.silverravenwolf.com.

deTraci Regula is the author of *The Mysteries of Isis* and coauthor of *Whispers of the Moon,* a biography of Scott Cunningham.

Janina Renée is the author of *Tarot Spells and Playful Magick.* She is currently studying herbs and healing, but her primary goal is learning to "affect the outcome of the day." In other words, she makes choices that create harmony with the universe's flow.

Sedwin is a writer and explorer of ancient Goddess spirituality. Based on the work of Marija Gimbutas, she has created and teaches the "Speaking the Language of the Goddess" workshop. She is currently working on a mystery novel that features a Wiccan heroine.

Cerridwen Iris Shea is an urban Witch, writer, tarot reader, and thoroughbred racing fan. She works backstage on a Broadway show and comes up with new spells in her cramped kitchen.

Maria Kay Simms is author of *The Witch's Circle*. A Wiccan High Priestess, she has also authored several astrology books and has been an astrologer for twenty-seven years. She holds professional certification from the National Council for Geocosmic Research (NCGR) and the American Federation of Astrologers. She is currently the elected Chair of the NCGR.

Martin Summerton is a Witch, astrologer, magician, and Qabalist. He is also a computer consultant specializing in DOS and other arcane systems.

Kala Trobe has been practicing spell-craft since an early age. Trial-and-error and unexpected side effects have taught her that concentrated will is the most important ingredient in any magic. She is author of the Llewellyn book *Invoke the Goddess* and lives in England.

Jim Weaver holds a degree in history and has had a lifelong interest in folk magic. He writes from his home deep in the Appalachian foothills, where he also paints in the American primitive style. He enjoys spending time in his herb and flower gardens.